"Mindfulness is made for introverts. In *The Awakened Introvert*, Arnie Kozak, PhD, provides you with simple steps to help you tap into your inner strengths and quiet the noise between your ears. You'll emerge with ninja-like powers to tap into the world's leading expert on 'all things you.' Quick tip: It starts with an inhale. You know what to do next. Then, without missing a beat, read Kozak's book."

> —**Nancy Ancowitz**, business communication coach and author
> of *Self-Promotion for Introverts*®

"*The Awakened Introvert* is the perfect answer to an introvert's need for solitude and sanctuary in a noisy world. Kozak's writing reflects the clarity and flow that introverts can achieve through the mindfulness exercises he weaves throughout the book. I highly recommend *The Awakened Introvert* for every introvert who wants to explore their inner world and emerge feeling more self-aware and at peace with who they are."

> —**Michaela Chung**, creator of Introvert Spring

"How can we be true to our deepest nature with so many claims on our time, senses, and energy? In *The Awakened Introvert*, psychologist and author Arnie Kozak offers a road map based on the teachings and practices of mindfulness that helps us stay connected to inner clarity, creativity, and peace in the midst of daily living."

> —**Tara Brach, PhD**, author of *Radical Acceptance* and *True Refuge*

"Arnie Kozak's merging of the two paradigms of introvertedness and awakening to the truths of one's existence is a potent reminder of how a thoughtful person can negotiate his or her way in a world fragmented by noise and chaos. Kozak has created an exciting new language to explore the same landscape of human dilemma that the Buddha spoke of. Hopefully more people can listen to this voice and benefit from the message it brings."

> —**Mu Soeng**, Buddhist scholar and author of *The Heart of the
> Universe* and other books

"This is a wonderful, practical guide for all those introverts (and extroverts as well) who need to be awakened to their boundless strengths. The author finishes what Susan Cain has begun with her best-selling *Quiet: The Power of Introverts in a World That Can't Stop Talking*. Arnie Kozak provides an extensive tapestry of 'quiet' exercises—mindfulness strategies, social communication skills, energy activities—that enrich self-care and self-restoration, and, most of all, boundless support for how to flourish as an introvert. After all, as the author points out, 'the Buddha was an introvert.' Arnie Kozak's book teaches us how to discover the introverted Buddha that lies within all human beings."

—**Robert J. Nash, EdD**, professor and Official University of Vermont Scholar in the Humanities, Social Sciences, and Creative Arts, director of the graduate Interdisciplinary Studies in Education program, and author of fifteen books and over one hundred scholarly articles

"Everyone can benefit from reading *The Awakened Introvert*. In the first part of the book, those of us who self-identify as extroverts will discover that our personalities also have introverted qualities. That's a revelation in itself! Then, through the use of multiple easy-to-learn mindfulness and cognitive behavioral exercises, the author shows us how to draw on the strengths of introversion to awaken to our full potential as human beings. This is a superb book!"

—**Toni Bernhard**, author of *How to Be Sick* and *How to Wake Up*

"Introversion is both a psychological attitude and a way of life. Those of us born introverted must take care not to feel too isolated, exhausted, and inferior or superior with our more extroverted friends, family, and society. Kozak does a superb job here offering us psychological and spiritual wisdom, practices, and research that allow us to engage with the best of what introversion can bring. This workbook is well written and easy to use. I strongly recommend it if you are an introvert or if you live with someone who is."

—**Polly Young-Eisendrath, PhD**, author of *The Present Heart: A Memoir of Love, Loss, and Discovery*

"Like so many introverts, I'd always sensed my introversion was a gift. But in those times when I tried to conform to an extrovert-driven world, I'd often lose faith in that intuition and feel flawed. Reading *The Awakened Introvert* has helped me trust my own instincts and deepened my mindfulness practice in surprising ways. I wish this book had been around twenty years ago (it would have saved me a lot of confusion), but I'm glad it's here now. I'd recommend it to any introvert—as well as any extrovert struggling to understand an introverted loved one."

—**Jaimal Yogis**, author of *Saltwater Buddha*, *The Fear Project*, and
the forthcoming Harper Collins memoir, *All Our Waves Are Water*

"There are two reasons why this book is important. The first is obvious: introverts can hugely benefit from the focus strategies provided here. The second reason is perhaps less obvious. After practicing mindfulness for a while, some people become hypersensitive and resistant to interacting with the 'normal world.' It's important to know that this is merely a temporary situation, an awkward intermediate stage between semi-coping (through tighten up and turn away) and super-coping (through open up and turn toward). Arnie's suggestions and encouragements can help speed people through that transition."

—**Shinzen Young**, author of *The Science of Enlightenment*

The
Awakened
Introvert

PRACTICAL MINDFULNESS SKILLS *to*
HELP YOU MAXIMIZE YOUR STRENGTHS
& THRIVE *in a* LOUD & CRAZY WORLD

Arnie Kozak, PhD

New Harbinger Publications, Inc.

Publisher's Note

This publication is designed to provide accurate and authoritative information in regard to the subject matter covered. It is sold with the understanding that the publisher is not engaged in rendering psychological, financial, legal, or other professional services. If expert assistance or counseling is needed, the services of a competent professional should be sought.

Excerpts from "East Coker" and "Little Gidding" from FOUR QUARTETS by T. S. Eliot. Copyright 1940, 1942 by T. S. Eliot; copyright © renewed 1968, 1970 by Esme Valerie Eliot and the Estate of T. S. Eliot. Reprinted by permission of Faber and Faber Ltd. and Houghton Mifflin Harcourt Publishing Company. All rights reserved.

Distributed in Canada by Raincoast Books

Copyright © 2015 by Arnie Kozak
       New Harbinger Publications, Inc.
       5674 Shattuck Avenue
       Oakland, CA 94609
       www.newharbinger.com

Cover design by Amy Shoup
Acquired by Wendy Millstine
Edited by Jean Blomquist

Library of Congress Cataloging-in-Publication Data on file

Printed in the United States of America

17   16   15

10   9   8   7   6   5   4   3   2   1   First printing

This book is dedicated to all the introverts in the world, especially my favorite one, Alexis.

Contents

Acknowledgments

A chain of events brought this book into being, and I'd like to thank those who made it possible. Wendy Millstine, acquisitions editor at New Harbinger, saw my program listing in the Kripalu Center for Yoga and Health and contacted me. I am grateful that she did. I would not have been in that catalog, teaching a workshop at Kripalu, without the support of Martha Williams, senior workshop programmer. Her support continues with my teaching of introvert and mindfulness workshops at Kripalu. My agent Grace Freedson got me the book contract to write *The Everything Guide to the Introvert Edge*, and initiated my path of writing for introverts. I'd also like to thank my fellow writing friend, artist, and introvert Erik Odin Cathcart for all his support. My way through the world is made more comfortable, soulful, and adventurous by my wife and favorite introvert, Alexis, who also read early drafts of these chapters. Thanks also to Hara Marano at *Psychology Today* for supporting my blog *The Buddha Was an Introvert*, and Sharon Kirk at Beliefnet for supporting my blog *Mindfulness Matters*, as well as to all the other authors writing for introverts, who have paved the way for this book.

Introduction

It's wonderful to be an introvert. You have the power of quiet, the edge of introspection, and the advantage of looking before you leap. However, despite the benefits of being an introvert, you may find yourself at odds with a society that has embraced extroversion as its ideal form of temperament. You may feel out of place and discriminated against—and you may be doing some of this discrimination! You may find that you are misunderstood, criticized, and underappreciated. You may also feel overwhelmed by the noise, commotion, and stress of everyday life.

This book will provide you with a comprehensive set of tools for understanding your introversion and making it work for you. You will learn about your unique introvert qualities and develop self-care strategies for the demands that you face in the world. These mindfulness-based strategies will help you to maximize your introvert strengths, and find balance both within yourself and without in the extrovert-dominated culture. Optimizing your introvert assets with the aid of mindfulness will help you to thrive, one moment at a time. Information is power and can lead to self-acceptance. You no longer have to apologize for being an introvert. You can awaken to your gifts. Mindfulness practice can also help you to awaken to your greater potential as a human being.

Introversion/extroversion is perhaps the most basic dimension of personality and the one that has been studied the most. Introverts can be distinguished from extroverts based on their tendencies and preferences in a number of domains, particularly how they handle social encounters. The crucial difference between introverts and extroverts is how stimulation is handled. Extroverts love, crave, and seek high levels of stimulation through activities, socializing, and taking risks. This is because their brains operate at lower levels of activation than introverts. Because introverts already have a higher level of activity in their brains, they can become overstimulated and perhaps even overwhelmed with the same level of stimulation that extroverts enjoy. Extroverts like to have many social contacts and tend to gain energy from these, while introverts feel drained by such contacts and prefer to limit them in number and quality. Introverts prefer a depth of interaction to small talk. The typical cocktail party that is unstructured, loud, and chaotic provides optimal stimulation for extroverts and overstimulation for introverts. Introverts and extroverts also differ in their concentration preferences. Introverts favor a quieter, more focused approach, taking up one thing at a time, while extroverts don't mind being interrupted and tend to engage multiple tasks simultaneously. The more that's going on, the better for extroverts, while introverts need a higher level of quiet, again because their brains are already more active than those of extroverts. Because of these differences, introverts have an acute need for solitude and quiet in their lives to rest, recharge, and restore their energy. Specific chapters will be devoted to the important themes of quiet, solitude, and energy.

Being an introvert can be like a double-edged sword. One side of this sword is a preference for the interior, a comfort with introspection, and a tendency to consider issues deeply. The other side of this sword is the tendency to be *so* thoughtful that it borders on stressful rumination, obsession, and preoccupation. The interior can be a place of insight or painful self-consciousness. It can be an abode of peace, ease, and acceptance, or it can be a place of judgment, self-criticism, and being stuck. Mindfulness is a sheath for the stressful side of the sword that you are likely to cut yourself on. Mindfulness prevents accidental cuts and also helps you to flourish in your life by empowering you to live focused on the present moment.

Another liability for introverts is energy management. Introverts need to recharge their batteries, especially when they are drained by prolonged contact in extroverted social situations. Typically, introverts need to withdraw into their safe interior spaces to restore their energy. Mindfulness gives them the ability to recharge more effectively when they withdraw as well as to be able to do some of this energy restoration on the fly as they are out participating in the world. By embracing mindfulness, you can increase your range of coping strategies, depth of focus, and resolve to thrive in the extrovert world on your own terms. You'll have more degrees of freedom, and when those terms are set by others, you will find mindfulness is a potent tool for helping you to adapt. With mindfulness, you can greet *any* situation with an ease of mind and a calmness of spirit.

Who This Workbook Is For

This workbook is for any introvert who feels challenged, overwhelmed, or stressed by the demands of living in an extrovert-dominated culture. You may find these stresses at home with your spouse and children, at work, or with your larger social network. It will also be useful for extroverts who may feel stressed by the hectic, relentless pace of life and want to develop their introverted qualities. All people are a mix of introvert and extrovert; no one is purely one way or the other. That said, it is still conventional to refer to "introverts" and "extroverts" for convenience, depending on the traits that prevail. This workbook will be especially useful for introverts who wish to learn more about using mindfulness to bring quiet, calm, and focus into their lives. Writer Anne Lamott (2013) recently said what could be considered an introvert's creed: "We work really hard at not being driven crazy by noise and speed and extremely annoying people, whose names we are too polite to mention" (3). Mindfulness can help you to not be driven crazy by the people, situations, and hectic pace of your life. Mindfulness is the gateway to freedom from dissatisfaction, anguish, and limitation.

How to Use This Workbook

Each chapter of this book can be read on its own. However, you will get the maximum benefit if you first read it all the way through. You can then go back and review the chapters and practices that resonated with you the most. Included in each chapter are mindfulness meditation practices followed by sections where you can reflect and write about the practices. Formal meditation practices require that you do nothing other than that practice for a designated period of time. Formal practices can be practiced on a regular basis. For each practice presented in the book, do the practice daily, and, if possible, for at least two weeks. There are seven formal practices and four informal practices presented throughout the book, as well as one exercise that can be done both formally and informally. You won't have the time to do all the practices at the same time, nor would you want to. Try each one and find the one or two that speak to you the most and then dedicate yourself to those. The intention of a daily practice typically translates into near daily in actual application. Informal mindfulness practices are meditation exercises that piggyback on other daily activities such as exercise, housework, and daily grooming. These exercises aim at engaging a different kind of attention as you go through your day and won't require extra time to practice. I offer selected stories (including some of my own) about introverts dealing with the challenges of the extroverted culture as well as a variety of written and monitoring exercises designed to build your awareness. Some of these exercises are available in downloadable format at the website associated with this book: http://www.newharbinger.com/36101. (See the very back of this book for more information.)

Gifts and Challenges of Being an Introvert

This workbook will encourage you to think about many facets of your life. You can start now by reflecting on the things you value most about being an introvert.

_____

_____

Now reflect on the situations that you find most challenging.

_____

_____

I could thrive in my life if I could change:

_____

_____

My Story: Greetings from a Card-Carrying Introvert

"Oh, no, not another holiday party," I sigh as I leave work on a Friday night. I arrive one and a half hours after the designated start time, hoping to find the party well underway. If it is, my arrival will be less conspicuous. I can survey the landscape unobtrusively, figuring out where I want to situate myself. Despite my attempt to arrive New York–fashion late, I am one of the first to arrive. It's that awkward in-between amount of people—not too few, not too many. I am conspicuous; there's nowhere to hide. I say hello to the host and do a quick inventory of the guests. To my chagrin, I don't know anyone else there. This is precisely the scenario I wished to avoid. This is exactly the situation that sits squarely outside my comfort zone.

I pour a glass of wine, fill my plate with food, and stand around self-consciously waiting for something to shift. After what seems an eternity, I recognize some guests who have just arrived. We start a conversation. It becomes animated. I relax. I start to feel at home in my surroundings and in my own skin. It turns out to be an enjoyable party. Many more people arrive, and it peaks hours after I thought it would. I have four substantial, meaningful, and enjoyable conversations. I leave feeling full, and not just because my belly is full of great food. My heart feels gratified, too; I've connected with people. If I don't "eat" tomorrow, I'll be fine. My quota for social nourishment has been satisfied. The party—as all parties are—was work for me; it required effort. I'm glad that I made the effort this evening. It was good to go.

Introverts Can Thrive in an Extroverted World

It is ironic that I've constructed a very public life for myself. My principal occupation is psychotherapist. I spend many hours a week sitting face-to-face with people having conversations. My secondary occupation is teacher. I conduct courses at the University of Vermont, the University of Vermont College of Medicine, the Barre Center for Buddhist Studies, and the Kripalu Center for Yoga and Health. I am "on" for hours at a time, lecturing, facilitating conversations, and guiding students in contemplative practices. I am also an author, and writing affords me welcomed solitude, quiet, and respite from the social aspects of my days. Yet writing, too, demands that I be public. Book signings, workshops, and interviews are all part of the territory. I am an introvert living, and now thriving, in an extrovert world.

I studied introversion in college and graduate school. I've always known that I am an introvert explicitly and implicitly. Yet, I never really considered that I lived in such an extroverted world—that somehow the extroversion had become the standard for behavior in this culture. Feeling bad about myself has often emerged in this gap between my introvert predilections and the reality of the world around me. Sometimes my quiet, observing demeanor makes people uncomfortable, especially if they know I'm a psychologist. They imagine I am analyzing them. (Don't worry—I'm not working unless you are paying me!) I've often been encouraged to be more outgoing, to put forth a more positive energy. I have felt guilty for not participating more and, even worse, I have felt shame for being the way I am. These feelings of inadequacy stemmed from buying into the extrovert standard and not appreciating that my introversion was a set of strengths, not liabilities. In the years since I have started writing about introversion, I have seen a transformation of my attitudes. I have been able to leverage my long-term contemplative practice of mindfulness as a potent tool to amplify this transformation, and I am excited to have an opportunity to share it with you.

Chapter 1

Stranger in a Strange Land: Defining Introversion

This chapter will explore what it means to be an introvert from a personality, psychological, and societal perspective. It will debunk myths related to introversion and help you to better appreciate your particular way of being in the world. You will have an opportunity to confirm your introversion and to understand the relationship between introversion and extroversion. The strengths and vulnerabilities of introverts will also be explored.

Introverts Are Not Failed Extroverts

There is nothing wrong with introversion, yet living in an extrovert-dominated culture can make you question your strengths as an introvert. You may find yourself out of balance trying to keep up with the extroverted pace of life. You may have lost touch with your values of quiet, solitude, and depth. This workbook will help you maximize your introvert qualities and inoculate you against living in the extrovert culture. You can think of this workbook as a manual for thriving in the challenging environment of contemporary, technologically dominated culture. Social media offers a safe and selective way for introverts to interact; you can participate when and where you'd like. Yet the same technology brings increased accessibility and expectations that you should always be on, available, and responsive. Even though you can participate with social media when you like, there are still expectations for you to share. It is hard to maintain a sense of peace in these arenas, too. The stimulating wealth of information available on the Internet may be fun for extroverts but can be overwhelming to introverts.

Introverts are not failed extroverts. The time has come for this culture to embrace the quiet strengths of introverts. If you have been disempowered, the tools in this workbook will empower you to be who you are without apology.

Signs of Being a Disempowered Introvert

Answer the following statements as true or false:

T   F   People have called me a loner or misanthrope, or antisocial or asocial, when I feel like doing something alone, by myself.

T   F   I feel guilty about letting people down when I don't feel like participating in the ways they would like me to participate.

T   F   I have often wondered if there is something wrong with me for feeling the way that I feel (for example, easily overwhelmed and drained in social situations).

T   F   I frequently feel like I am missing out on the good time that everyone else seems to be having.

If you have answered "true" to any of these statements, you may have lost touch with your introvert strengths, values, and direction. You may have bought into the larger culture's devotion to extroversion, a devotion that does not value a quiet, introspective life. The exercises and practices in this workbook will help you to reclaim your introvert values and to thrive among the extroverts.

Introvert Benefits, Tendencies, and Preferences

There is growing recognition that introverts have gotten a bad rap for a long time. Our culture has become fascinated with action-oriented, vocal people and has overlooked the valuable contribution of the quieter members of society. There are as many ways of being an introvert as there are introverts. How introverted are you? Here is a list of introvert benefits, tendencies, and preferences. Check off the ones that you see in yourself:

☐ I am thoughtful: I like to think things over before acting or speaking. I am more of a listener than a talker.

☐ I am introspective: I value ideas, imagination, and writing.

☐ I am deliberate: I take measured action instead of acting impulsively.

☐ I am focused: I like to hone in on one thing at a time. It's frustrating to be interrupted frequently.

☐ I am calm: I prefer being soft-spoken, low-key, and mellow.

☐ I am heedful: I am not a big risk taker.

☐ I am quiet: I don't talk unnecessarily.

☐ I am loyal: I have close, intimate connections with a small number of people.

☐ I prefer expressing myself through writing.

☐ I am self-sufficient: I can be content without a lot of entertainment and stimulation.

☐ I sometimes find it hard to think on the spot. I often think of something I would have liked to have said after the situation has passed.

☐ I am detail oriented.

☐ I enjoy having solitude on a regular basis.

☐ I prefer one-on-one or small group discussion to the brief, superficial conversations I might have at a party.

☐ I often let my phone go to voicemail; I'd prefer to send a text or e-mail.

☐ I prefer to survey a new situation from the outside before jumping in.

☐ I feel overstimulated in loud, chaotic environments and seek refuge by going outside or hiding out in the bathroom.

☐ I prefer a quiet night at home or at a restaurant to going out on the town.

☐ I feel drained after a lot of socializing.

☐ I have a high need for privacy.

The statements above are not a scientific survey to establish introversion. However, if you agree with many of these benefits, tendencies, and preferences, it's a good chance that your personality disposition is on the introverted side of the introvert-extrovert spectrum.

Where Are All the Introverts?

It may appear that extroverts, especially in the workplace, populate the world. The introverts that do stand out are likely at the far extreme of introversion and may come across as misanthropic loners. Laurie Helgoe (2013) reports that when you measure introversion and extroversion through the Myers-Briggs Type Indicator (a personality inventory based on the theories of psychoanalyst Carl Jung), studies suggest that half the population are introverts. There are several reasons that introverts are not more prominent in this culture:

1. Introverts are invisible. Our culture is extrovert dominated; that is the ideal. The extrovert is celebrated in public life (almost all presidents have been extroverts) and in the media. Our culture says be bold, take risks, and be assertive, which often means be loud, aggressive, or daring. Introverts get overlooked or pushed aside (Cain 2012).

2. Not every introvert is an "introvert." Most people are clustered around the middle, meaning they are a balance of introvert and extrovert (see "Most Introverts and Extroverts Cluster Around the Middle" later in this chapter). Some fall on the side of being predominately introvert and some fall on the side of being predominately extrovert. These people won't look like the extremes portrayed in books and other media.

3. Many introverts behave like extroverts and are therefore *pseudoextroverts*. This practice can be called *extroverting*. These introverts may not realize that they are introverts and that there is another way to conduct themselves.

The apparent superiority in numbers of extroverts does not mean that everyone is truly extroverted. Introverts are more prevalent than you may realize.

Differentiating Introversion from Clinical and Other Conditions

There can be a superficial resemblance between some of the things introverts do with some of the things people with clinical and other conditions do. Unless you've been trained in psychology, you might not realize the differences. The biggest confusion arises between introversion and shyness—a condition where a person wants to be social but is inhibited due to anxiety. You can be a shy introvert or a shy extrovert. Most introverts are not shy, even though they may look that way when they avoid or are uncomfortable with certain kinds of social situations, such as being forced to make small talk. Introversion is grounded in personality, while shyness is a treatable condition. Put another way, shyness is a problem, not a preference. Fortunately, there is no cure for introversion! And, of course, there doesn't need to be, since there is nothing wrong with being an introvert.

When your energy is drained from too much socializing and not enough recovery time, you may look and feel depressed. However, unlike clinical depression, your condition is transient and will reverse itself once you have reconstituted your energy. Depression will always involve either sadness or a lack of interest in pleasure that persists for at least two weeks. It is also accompanied by other symptoms, such as changes in appetite, sleep patterns, weight gain or loss, fatigue, confusion, trouble making decisions, memory difficulties, feelings of low self-worth or value, or suicidal thoughts. If your fatigue does not respond to some good introvert restoration and if your desire to withdraw from people is not just a necessary tactic to recharge your batteries, you may want to see your primary care provider or a mental health professional to be evaluated for depression.

A preference for occasional solitude is a hallmark of introverts. There is a condition called schizoid personality disorder where the tendency toward solitude is taken to the extreme of isolation. Whereas as an introvert you may choose, at times, to withdraw from social situations, people with schizoid personality disorder may not be capable of connecting with others. Unfortunately, the term "introvert" has, in the past, been used in official diagnostic criteria for schizoid personality disorder. Advocacy by introvert writers has helped to get this language removed from current diagnostic criteria.

There is significant overlap between introversion and the concept of the highly sensitive person (HSP). HSPs are highly sensitive to stimulation in their environment, including the emotions of other people. They tend not to like noises, commotion, and stimulants like caffeine. Introverts make up 80 percent of HSPs, and 20 percent of the population is believed to be HSPs (Aron 1997). If you are one of the approximately 16 percent of the population who is an introverted HSP, you will have particular self-care requirements and challenges. Quiet, solitude, and proactive energy management will be key components of self-care. You will find chapters devoted to each of these topics later in this book.

What's in a Label? Dimensions of Personality

Human beings are complex, and while it is tempting (and gratifying) to reduce this complexity to simple dimensions such as "introvert" versus "extrovert," this doesn't reflect nature. Introversion-extroversion is one of a handful of basic dimensions of personality, but most discussions of introversion-extroversion ignore the other, very relevant personality dimensions, such as emotional stability (or neuroticism), openness to experience, and others (see "Measuring Introversion and Extroversion" later in this chapter). You may be familiar with the notion that people are either dominantly left-brained (meaning logic and language dominated) or right-brained (creative and emotion dominated). This simplification is based more on myth than reality. Nielson and colleagues (2013) provide compelling evidence that there is no scientific basis for the left-brain, right-brain difference between people. However, people do vary in how introverted and extroverted they are. Still, these differences exist on a continuum, and how introverted or extroverted you will be in any given situation is a function of situation, not just your inborn temperament.

You can think of the label of "introvert" as a description of your center of gravity when it comes to responding to situations. Personality descriptions like introvert and extrovert describe *response tendencies*—that is, characteristic ways of reacting to a situation. Personality is just that—a tendency. It is not fixed, irrevocable, or immutable. It is how you are *likely* to respond in a given situation. But awareness can change your response, and this workbook is dedicated to raising awareness of your introvert tendencies.

Introvert and extrovert traits provide shortcuts for navigating through the onslaught of energy and information that you encounter. Personality provides shortcuts that help you to cope in the world in automatic ways. You don't have to think about everything, you can just act. The introvert will be prone to hesitate before acting; the extrovert will be prone to act first. These are the basic response tendencies.

Throughout the rest of this book, the term "introvert" is used as shorthand for the more precise "people with an introvert center of gravity who demonstrate a greater frequency and preference for introverted traits." The term "extrovert" is shorthand for "people with an extrovert center of gravity who demonstrate a greater frequency and preference for extroverted traits."

Most Introverts and Extroverts Cluster Around the Middle

Many things are distributed in the "normal curve." The normal curve is a statistical term for the familiar bell-shaped curve that appears when things like average height or the prevalence of certain personality are graphed. Most people, whether it is height or personality being measured, will be clustered around the middle—the average—and then trail off at the extremes. As I mentioned earlier, introversion and extroversion are no exception (Zelenski, Whelan, Nealis, et al. 2013). The normal curve can be useful for understanding introverts and extroverts in a larger context and also appreciating the literature on introverts and extroverts. The normal curve predicts that, on the average, about two-thirds of the population will be centered around the middle. One-sixth will be more strongly introverted; the other sixth will be more intensely extroverted. When you read about introverts and extroverts, authors typically describe the more extreme cases. Everyone, even extreme introverts and extroverts, contains some quality of the other in some situations. It can be useful to know that most people are around average. This can help to offset an "us" versus "them" mentality. The challenge of being an introvert is to honor, accept, and celebrate your introverted qualities and to develop your extrovert qualities, which you will likely need to engage from time to time. It is best not to think of yourself and others as strictly introverts or extroverts. Extreme cases are useful for highlighting differences, but at the same time, they tend to exaggerate these differences.

Measuring Introversion and Extroversion

If you look at the research literature, most of the studies on introversion and extroversion (you'll see it spelled "extraversion" in research studies) use the NEO (Neuroticism-Extraversion-Openness) Personality Inventory. The NEO measures the "big five" dimensions of personality: extroversion, neuroticism or emotional stability, openness to experience, agreeableness, and conscientiousness. Subjects who take this inventory vary in how extroverted they are. The inventory does not distinguish between introverts and extroverts but rather places subjects on a continuum of more or less extroversion. The way this inventory was designed has implications for introverts. Extroversion is set as the benchmark and is characterized by high-arousal positive emotions such as excitement, gregariousness, and stimulation-seeking. If you score low in this inventory, presumably you are an introvert, yet the adjectives used to describe low scorers are "reserved, sober, unexuberant, aloof, task oriented, retiring, and quiet." These adjectives make introverts seem less desirable than the "optimistic, affectionate, and fun-loving" extroverts. It is not clear how scoring high or low on the scale of extroversion corresponds to real-world differences between introverts and extroverts. Despite the limitations of the terms, this inventory likely taps into some of the differences between introverts and extroverts. An all-or-nothing mentality does not fit here, and the difference between introverts and extroverts is not what behaviors they enjoy but how frequently they enjoy them. According to Fleeson and Gallagher (2009), sociability, boldness, and activity are not owned by extroverts. Introverts also will engage in these behaviors, just less frequently than extroverts.

The difference between "introverts" and "extroverts," then, is the frequency with which they exhibit introverted and extroverted behaviors. In the research literature (and in this book, too, for the sake of convenience), people are referred to as "introverts" or "extroverts," but this is misleading. There is no such thing as an "introvert"—only people who think, feel, and behave like introverts most of the time; and there is no such thing as an "extrovert"—only people who think, feel, and behave like extroverts most of the time. Both introverts and extroverts (except at the very extremes) have a repertoire of both introverted and extroverted tendencies. If you measure a group of people on the trait of extroversion, split the group in half, and then look at differences between them, you probably won't find any. To compensate for this, researchers will take the extremes at either end (that is, the top and bottom 25 percent) and compare them (Blumenthal 2001). Therefore, research doesn't represent everyone.

There is, however, a quick way to determine whether you are an introvert or an extrovert from this research perspective. Gosling and colleagues (2003), who did not always have the time to do a complete NEO assessment, developed the Ten Item Personality Inventory (TIPI). In it, there are two statements devoted to introversion and extroversion:

"I see myself as reserved, quiet."

Strongly Disagree	Moderately Disagree	Disagree a Little	Neither Agree nor Disagree	Agree a Little	Moderately Agree	Strongly Agree
1	2	3	4	5	6	7

"I see myself as extraverted, enthusiastic."

Strongly Disagree	Moderately Disagree	Disagree a Little	Neither Agree nor Disagree	Agree a Little	Moderately Agree	Strongly Agree
7	6	5	4	3	2	1

You rate your level of agreement or disagreement with these two statements, then add the two scores together. A score of 8 would put you right in the middle. Scores higher than 8 put you in introvert territory and scores lower than 8 put you in extrovert territory.

What was your score? _____

Another popular measure of introversion/extroversion is the Myers-Briggs Type Indicator (MBTI), which, as I mentioned before, is based on the theory of the pioneering psychoanalyst Carl Jung. The MBTI has been used more in human resource contexts, while the NEO has more frequently been used in a research context. Studies that have looked at the overlap between the MBTI and the NEO find significant but not complete overlap (Furnham, Moutafi, and Crump 2003). The MBTI has a more positive view of introversion and characterizes introverts as preferring the inner world of ideas and gaining energy from the images, thoughts, and memories found there. They are most comfortable with solitude or one-on-one interactions. They value reflection and seek clarity before jumping into action. Ideas can sometimes be more compelling than the reality they represent.

A Quick Look into the Brain

Johnson and colleagues (1999) conducted a brain imaging study with people who measured high and low in a measure of extroversion on the NEO Personality Inventory. They found significant differences in the patterns of blood flow. Introverts had higher blood flow in their frontal lobes—the place where narrative-based thinking, or "self-talk," occurs. This suggests that introverts are more in their "heads" than extroverts, who are more oriented to their senses and action, which is reflected in their need for stimulation. These findings should not be interpreted to mean that blood flow in the particular brain regions was absent for extroverts, nor do they mean that blood flow in other brain regions associated with extroversion was absent for introverts. Rather, it shows that blood flow was more or less robust to the extent that it can be measured. These differences are a matter of degree and may be helpful for understanding the differences that are found between introverts and extroverts.

Awakening as an Introvert: Using Mindfulness for Self-Care

To be an awakened introvert, you respect your unique introvert qualities while not succumbing to cultural biases against introverts. Mindfulness, as will be discussed in the next chapter and throughout this workbook, will help you to expand your possibilities as an introvert. Mindfulness is not a tool for making you more like an extrovert; rather, it can help you be more comfortable, adaptable, and flexible as an introvert. Mindfulness skills can enhance, optimize, and expand your ability to be at peace in the most trying situations in your life, especially those situations that are taxing, such as being "on" at work, communicating with extroverts, and dealing with the constant interruptions of daily life. You may be challenged to maintain privacy in a world that is becoming less and less private. You may be confronted with an environment of ceaseless noise, commotion, and triviality. You may be exposed to an overabundance of energy-draining situations on a daily basis.

The good news is that you bring to these challenges a deep well of introspection, the power of quiet, and a comfort with silence, stillness, and repose. These advantages, however, have some blind spots—a vulnerability to being too much in your head, losing touch with your body and your surroundings, and feeling overwhelmed by stress in situations that are overstimulating. Mindfulness can help to temper these vulnerabilities and open your blind spots.

Here are some signs that you have gotten out of balance:

- You may find that your energy is low: you feel tired, sluggish, and heavy.

- Your thinking is slower than usual: you have trouble concentrating, finding words, and making decisions.

- You may feel tense, stressed, frazzled, or overwhelmed.

- You want to withdraw, hide under the covers, and not talk.

- Other: _____

Marti Olsen Laney (2007) correctly encourages her readers to "accept your internal conflicts by tolerating discomfort and confusion" (104). The list above can be seen as examples of these discomforts and confusions. Laney's admonition is easier said than done. Intentions may not be enough to increase your ability to accept these conflicts. If you experience any of these signs of imbalance, you can use the mindfulness practices in this book to start the process of bringing yourself into balance. Since mindfulness practice helps to build skills, it can help you to clarify the situations where you need to protect yourself, test your limits, accept what is happening, or modify your environment. These considerations remind me of a story about how skills training and mindfulness practice helped me when I was faced with a conflict between taking care of myself and meeting the expectations of others—a very common conflict for us introverts.

My Story: Prioritizing Self-Care over Meeting Expectations

I was teaching a workshop for the Vermont Psychological Association entitled "The Mindful Introvert: Contemplative Practices for Self-Care and Burnout." I was teaching fellow clinicians, many of whom were introverts, how to best serve their introvert patients and take care of themselves in the process. Mindfulness is a key to this self- and other care. These workshops have a standard format. They meet for an entire day at a hotel with a luncheon between the morning and afternoon sessions. Participants sit around the table in groups of eight or ten. I have always loathed these luncheons because I am forced into conversation with the person to my left or right, and sometimes find it difficult to navigate this territory. What do we talk about? The weather? That seems so superficial. If not the weather, what then? Do I interview this person and find out who they are? That can be interesting and exhausting. The luncheons are stressful events, even when I am just a participant in one of these workshops. This day, since I was presenting, the stress would be amplified.

Since I was teaching introvert self-care, I decided that I would practice what I preach. During the morning session, I announced to the group that I would not be with them at lunch. I explained that this is what I needed to do in order to take care of my energy. It was nothing personal. I knew that this day was going to be a big drain on my energy and the added lunch event would only make things worse.

So, indeed, I did exactly what I said I would do—I skipped the luncheon. I went down the street to a restaurant, sat at the bar with my laptop, and enjoyed my lunch in quiet. After lunch, I did some mindful walking around Montpelier. I returned to the workshop more refreshed than I would have been if I had sat through the luncheon. The keys to this act of self-care were (1) recognizing that self-care was at issue and (2) giving myself permission to take care of myself in the way that I knew I had to.

I hope that this story can inspire you to take care of yourself in the situations that you find taxing. In fact, you can consider this entire book a giant permission slip to help you to do the things you need to do to take care of yourself—without guilt.

Concluding Thoughts

We each have a center of gravity that is determined by temperament and learning. If you are an introvert and are forced to behave like an extrovert in some aspects of your life, you may not even realize where your center of gravity is. The quiet and body-based practices of mindfulness can help you to discover this comfortable center. The exercises in this workbook will help you to arrange your life in harmony with your center of gravity. At the same time, you don't want to do this slavishly. Mindfulness exercises can help you both to expand the range of where you can function and to decrease the recovery time from excursions outside your comfort zone that take you away from your center of gravity.

Neuroscientists have recently discovered that the human brain is very plastic—meaning that it changes in response to experience. So, whenever you learn something new, whenever you expand your range or move outside of your comfort zone, your brain is growing new connections. Many scientific studies have shown that mindfulness meditation promotes neuroplasticity—that is, the ability to grow new neurons and connections in the brain. You, too, can learn to promote changes in your brain, and mindfulness, as we will see in the next chapter, is key to this transformation.

Chapter 2

Mindfulness 101

Mindfulness is an indispensable tool for introverts. This chapter will provide a basic introduction to the concept, practice, and application of mindfulness—a field manual, if you will, for living in the present moment. Learning how to dwell in the here and now is a skill that can change your life. Your introvert quality of introspection makes mindfulness a natural fit, since mindfulness meditation helps you to become intimate with your interior in a way that transcends introspection. Mindfulness can help you to transform your relationship to thinking and move cognition away from rumination, obsession, and preoccupation, which are the downsides of introspection, toward flexibility, openness, and peace. The skills and practices of mindfulness can be the foundation for embracing your strengths, maintaining balance, and thriving in your life.

What Is Mindfulness?

When you consider the term "mindfulness," there is an interesting play on words. Typically, the mind is "full" of thoughts, memories, and stories, yet mindfulness refers to a mind that is *not* pursuing the collection of these mental things. To be mindful is not to rid your mind of thinking but rather to bring awareness to what is happening in your mind—in other words, the *process* of what is happening in your mind in the moment.

There is a popular cartoon that shows a man with a huge thought bubble above his head, filled with intricate patterns. Next to this image is the same man with an empty speech bubble coming out of his mouth. The caption reads, "What I think; what I say." This is likely a familiar phenomenon for you. Your head is busy, but this may not translate into talking. That richness goes on in the interior, and the people around you may have no idea that you are thinking so much or so deeply about things.

There is another cartoon that shows a man walking with his dog. The thought bubble above the man depicts people, cars, noise, bills, technology, and much more. The thought bubble above the dog's head shows the scene they are walking through, two trees, and the sun above. The caption reads, "Mind Full, or Mindful?"

The awakened introvert bridges these two worlds, moving closer to the dog's-eye view of the world. Mindfulness provides opportunities to simply be with the experience in the moment, without adding commentary or being distracted. If you are walking, for example, this involves the action of walking along with the sensory experiences of walking. Mindfulness practice helps you become friends with your mind.

Mindfulness depends on the quality of attention in any given moment. Typically, the mind is engaged in telling stories featuring the self—the story of me. In other words, the *content* or story line of the mind in the moment is this: *What am I doing? Where am I going? What do people think of me? What's coming up next?* You can spend almost your entire life caught up in these self-referential dialogues. When you can set aside the stories and attend to the experience happening now, you have moved into the nontypical awareness called mindfulness. As an introvert, you are likely very familiar with this internal-talk space; it may be where you spend a lot of your time. Mindfulness can help you to get out of these conversations at will, especially when they turn negative.

Neuroscientists such as Brewer (2011) call this tendency toward self-referential talk the *default mode network* (DMN) of the brain. If your brain were imaged as you engaged in the DMN, it would show a characteristic pattern of activation in two key brain regions: the medial prefrontal cortex (mPFC), which is involved in social and autobiographical awareness, and the posterior cingulate cortex (PCC), which is involved with memory retrieval, among other things. When you engage mindfulness, your attention comes out of the DMN and into the present moment. When you become mindful, the activity in the DMN stops and another pattern of brain activation emerges that is more focused on sensory and bodily experiences.

The Default Mode Network (DMN): Your Brain on Talk

When you are in the DMN, your attention can go to the past, present, or future and have a positive, neutral, or negative tone. This creates a three-by-three grid of possibilities like a tic-tac-toe board (see the figure that follows). Throughout the rest of your day, stop yourself and see if the DMN is active. Are you fantasizing about the future? If it is a pleasant fantasy, you are in the upper right sector, in "anticipation." If it is unpleasant, you are in the lower right sector of "worry." Are you reviewing something that happened in the past? Are you generating an opinion about this present moment—perhaps liking or disliking what is happening? Often the DMN is just in a neutral place—neither pleasant nor unpleasant. Thoughts, recollections, and images from the past and future may arise, but they lack an emotional charge. When the neutral zone is in the present tense, there is commentary about the present moment that also lacks an emotional charge. For example, there could be an ongoing narration of experience. You say to yourself, *There is a red pickup. I think that's a Ford. I wonder what year that is?* This can seem like mindfulness, but it is different, because the mind is still talking and generating opinions about what is happening in the present without experiencing it fully. Mindfulness does not have the "voice-over" of experience.

	PAST	**PRESENT**	**FUTURE**
PLEASANT	Reverie	"I like…"	Anticipation
NEITHER PLEASANT NOR UNPLEASANT	Neutral	Neutral	Neutral
UNPLEASANT	Rumination	"I don't like…"	Worry

The topography of the default mode network.

The Geography of Now

The alternative to the DMN is the here and now. The present moment is comprised of sensory experiences: what you see, hear, sense in the body, taste, and smell. According to meditation teacher Shinzen Young (2005), these are the objective or outer senses. You can also have subjective or inner senses. These include the self-talk of the DMN, images that appear on the mind's screen, and emotional feelings. The present moment is also comprised of some action or activity: reading, walking, sitting, talking, and so on. When your full attention is with your senses and the activity of the moment, you are being mindful. You can also be mindful of the interior senses, but this is trickier. It is possible to be aware of the fact that you are thinking—in other words, you can be mindful that your attention was just lost in a story or that a story is present without engaging in the content of that story or pursuing it further. This is a more challenging mindfulness practice: to become aware of what is happening in the mind as *processes* rather than *contents*. When the mind is engaged in a story, it tends to elaborate and "persist" that story. Instead of just acknowledging the presence of the story, the mind runs with it—reviewing it, adding details, and perhaps repeating the story over and over again. The mind proliferates the story. With mindfulness comes the choice of extricating yourself from that story, interrupting its proliferation to bring you into the present moment.

If, after monitoring your DMN, you find that you are almost always on the top shelf of the tic-tac-toe board having pleasant memories, satisfaction, and anticipation, then you might not find mindfulness practice all that compelling. If, as is more likely the case, you often find yourself on the bottom shelf contending with regret, dissatisfaction, and worry, then mindfulness will be of great value to you. A cartoon in *The New Yorker* once showed a beleaguered-looking husband being comforted by his attentive wife. She tells him, "You should never engage in unsupervised introspection." The man is clearly spending time on the bottom shelf. The introvert mind, in particular, may be prone to focusing on the past or the future. It can be hard to get out of your head. Your mind wants to process things deeply. Thinking is a comfortable place and you may not realize to what extent you spend time in the negative spaces. Mindfulness is the supervision your mind needs.

The DMN has a penchant for getting you into trouble. It can spin stories of envy, fear, and self-pity. It can make you feel self-consciousness, self-loathing, and self-doubt. Another point of trouble is that it removes you from your experiences. If you've ever watched the director's commentary on a DVD, you will have noticed that the director's voice, along with that of an actor or producer, talks over the movie, which recedes into the background. The DMN is just like the director's commentary. It talks over the movie of your life. The movie that is your life is there, but its volume is reduced and its intensity diminished. Mindfulness can help you to clear away the internal talk and experience your life in vivid color, brilliant sound, and clear bodily feelings.

Many minds have an obsessional tendency. This can be a particular problem for introverts. Mindfulness practice engages the mind's tendency to obsess and puts it to good use. Instead of thinking *Why is this terrible thing happening to me?* with all of that question's attendant worries, the mind says with curiosity, *This is happening.* For example, on the coldest day of winter, you return home from an out-of-town trip to find your home ice-cold. You can see your breath as you move through the house. You discover that you have run out of heating fuel oil. It is late Friday afternoon and the fuel company is about to close. Your mind races with thoughts like these: *How could I be so stupid to let this happen? Oh my god, the pipes are going to freeze! My plans for the evening are ruined; this is terrible.* These thoughts reflect the DMN doing its thing. Mindfulness brings attention, interest, and action to the situation. Mindfulness says, *This is happening… How do I best deal with it?* This thought is absent the drama of the other thoughts. It is pragmatic and focused. Next, you call the fuel company, pay the emergency fuel delivery surcharge, and start a fire in the woodstove. The problem is addressed without the added anguish of DMN-type thoughts.

The Entire Universe in a Single Breath

Breathing is often the starting place for learning mindfulness, and you'll be receiving detailed instructions on the rationale and method for practice below. In fact, breathing meditation is what the soon-to-be Buddha practiced under the bodhi tree on the way to awakening twenty-five hundred years ago.

You can focus on just about anything for mindfulness practice, but the breath has some particular advantages. First, breathing is portable. You can't forget to bring it with you. And like the old ads for the American Express Card, you can't leave home without it. Breathing happens all on its own; you don't have to worry about it or work to control it. The most primitive part of the brain—the brain stem—controls breathing. This way, you can keep breathing while you are sleeping and even when you are in a coma. While the brain stem controls breathing, the limbic system, or the emotional center of the brain, influences each breath you take. If you are anxious, your breathing will reflect this. If you are feeling good, your breathing will reflect that. Finally, your rational brain can influence breathing, too. You can decide to hold your breath, take a deep breath, or breathe rapidly. Since breathing is an automatic process, some people notice a slight twinge of self-consciousness when they start to pay attention to it. It's like asking a centipede how he walks. He didn't have to think about it, and now that he has to think about it, he may start tripping over his feet. If you start thinking too much about how to breathe, just relax and try not to control it. Just pay attention to how it is; your body will take care of the rest.

Another advantage is that breathing is embodied. Breathing is always different and you can start to appreciate these differences by noticing the variations in your breathing. When the historical Buddha meditated under the tree of awakening, he focused on his breathing, noting that the breath could be long or short on the inhalation or exhalation. For your part, you can feel the connection of the breath to the entire body, or you can feel it just at one point. Attention to breathing may give rise to pleasure, even rapture. These are all things that can be noticed in the context of the pedestrian breath.

As you breathe, you will notice the DMN becoming active. It's easy to get caught up in its stories. It is also possible to notice the elaboration of the story as an event in the mind that can be treated with mindfulness, and from there to soothe the DMN with breathing awareness. You can feel your breath moving through the body and mind as a healing balm. All of this will happen as you breathe naturally. You don't have to breathe in any particular way. The breath will take care of itself.

The more you practice paying attention to your breathing, the more your mind may steady itself. This, however, is not an explicit aim of practice. If you try to fix the mind in place, that effort may actually get in the way. If, instead, you notice where the mind goes and gently bring it back each time it moves away, that action will steady the mind.

Other things will make themselves apparent as you breathe. One is the fact that each breath is different (just like all snowflakes are different when you examine them closely enough). Each breath has a different emotional flavoring. Each cycle of the breath has a unique energetic signature. Everything is always changing. You can experience this firsthand within your very own body.

You can also observe how your mind wants to hold on to things—to grasp, to cling, to get caught up in desire. You can notice how your mind wants things. Perhaps it wants your breathing to be relaxing, peaceful, and soothing. Perhaps it wants your mind to be quiet, compliant, and happy (at least that's how you believe your mind should be). Perhaps it wants the surrounding environment to be a certain way. Perhaps you are frustrated by noises around you. Perhaps you want certain conditions to prevail in your body: the itches, aches, and pains *shouldn't* be there. When you notice the mind reaching for things that it wants, you have an opportunity to come back into the moving energy of the breath. The nice thing about the breath is that it receives your attention no matter how long you've ignored it. It is always present doing its thing whether you express your gratitude or not. The breath is a portable sanctuary.

During a *Fresh Air* interview, the writer Anne Lamott cautioned that the word "should" is a red flag that a lie is about to be told. As you begin to meditate, be mindful of *shoulds* that are present. There is no right way to do this practice. The goal is not some particular outcome. So, the only thing that *should* happen is the application of attention over and over again. Just doing this is enough. Focusing on the practice itself rather than hoped-for results can help you to persevere and avoid frustration.

The whole universe is represented in the breath. The molecules of air that you are breathing in contain hydrogen, oxygen, carbon, and nitrogen atoms that were present when the universe began. The Latin root for *spirit* is the same root for *breathing*. You *inspire* and you *expire*. Breathing can connect you to everything else.

Formal Practice: *Breathing Meditation*

You can do breathing meditation anywhere or anytime. It is portable, since you are always breathing—and if you are not, coping in the extrovert world will be the least of your problems! You can pay attention to your breathing while sitting, walking, standing, and even when you are lying down. It helps to be comfortable, but it's not necessary to get too focused on posture. One guideline can help: keep your back straight. If you slump, your airway will have unnecessary pressure on it. Sitting with your back straight is a dignified, even noble, way to sit; with it, you communicate to yourself that you are giving your best effort to this practice. Sit comfortably. You can fold your legs one on top of the other or one in front of the other and make sure your hips sit above your knees, courtesy of a cushion or a chair. Not everyone can fold their legs over so that they touch the mat. If your knees are high up from the floor, you might want to place a couple of cushions under your floating knees to give them support. In one style, you fold your right leg in front of your left leg (or the reverse, if you prefer). In another style, you place your right foot on your left thigh (this is called half-lotus).

You can also do the practice sitting in a chair. It's recommended that you place your feet flat on the floor in front of you and sit with your back straight to keep the breath flowing. You can do this practice with your eyes open or closed, whichever is most comfortable for you. If you keep your eyes open, maintain a soft gaze without focusing on anything intently.

You might want to begin by doing a quick inventory of everything that is present in your body and mind. Think about the tic-tac-toe board, and the nine sectors of the DMN it presents—past, present, and future, either pleasant, unpleasant, or neutral— and the internal and external senses. What sounds are present? What do you see? (Even with your eyes closed, you can see patterns of shadow and light.) Do you smell or taste anything? What can you feel in your body? You can always notice the sensations that arise as your butt makes contact with the cushion or chair. What other sensations are present? Make a mental note of all these sensations as if you were a scientist making observations, just making some quick notes on a clipboard.

Once you have done this quick inventory, begin focusing your attention on the process of your breathing. You can bring your focus to a narrow point at the tip of the nose or follow the movement of air from the tip of the nose through the entire apparatus of breathing—through the nose, throat, chest, and abdomen. You are looking for the physical sensations that are present in the moment. Breathe naturally and try to receive what is present, rather than trying to make the breathing or the sensations the way you think they should be.

Within a few seconds, you will notice that your attention will move back into one of the nine sectors of the DMN. This is fine. It does not indicate a problem with your mind. Attention wanders with all minds, especially when they are beginning meditation. Your job is to gently escort your attention back to the breath sensations that are present now. These will, of course, be different from the ones that were present before your attention moved away. Repeat this process over and over again. This is the key action of mindfulness meditation. When your attention moves away, you bring it back. The goal is not to try to keep your attention still, but to develop the skill to return attention whenever it has wandered away.

That's it. The instructions are simple. The practice is straightforward. It may not be easy to keep your attention on the breath, but if you can let go of the idea of how your attention and breathing should be, you will be on your way to enjoying and benefiting from practice. Start with a five- or ten-minute practice and work your way up to twenty minutes or more for each sitting session.

Meditation Reflection

Take a few moments to reflect on what came up for you during this practice. What did you learn about yourself? What thoughts, emotions, and bodily sensations were most prominent, interesting, or surprising?

_____

_____

_____

_____

Where Does the Mind Go and Why Does It Go There?

Where do you spend most of your time? You've noticed that attention has a tendency to wander from the present moment, so you can also ask *why* attention moves away. What is it seeking? What does it want? Do you really need what the mind thinks it needs?

	PAST	PRESENT	FUTURE
PLEASANT			
NEITHER PLEASANT NOR UNPLEASANT			
UNPLEASANT			

Spend a few minutes doing mindfulness of the breath. When attention moves away to past, future, or commentary on the present, ask yourself, *What does my mind want?* You'll find the usual suspects here. The mind wants reassurance, comfort, distraction, entertainment, and validation. What else is true for you? Write your answers in the grid above. Once you've identified what your mind is seeking, you can further contemplate these questions: Is it necessary? Can it wait? Is the desire a habit, done compulsively and without thinking? Can you let it go? What did you discover when monitoring your thoughts in this way? Write in the spaces below.

_____

_____

_____

_____

The mind has its habits of moving away from the present moment. It loves to voice-over the present with opinions and to envision the future and review the past, separating you from the experience of the present moment. For each one of these excursions from the present moment, there is a motivation. A little bit of investigating can reveal these motivations. Once they are uncovered, you can then begin the process of letting them go. Mindfulness is a vote of confidence in yourself, and a lack of mindfulness is, likewise, a vote of no confidence. For example, anxiety says, "I must think about this future event over and over to prepare for it, get it right, and avoid disaster." The anxiety views your life out of context. When you look at your life *in* context, you can find countless instances where you have handled present-moment challenges successfully. Mindfulness reestablishes confidence by telling the anxious tendencies of the mind that when that future moment becomes the present moment, you will handle it. Therefore, you don't need to obsess over that situation now, and you can return your attention to a peaceful abiding with the sensations of the present moment. This is your introvert mind at its best.

Levels of Awareness

Different levels of awareness can prevail at any moment. There is the level of automatic pilot, or what we might call *reactive without awareness*. This is the default setting of awareness and reflects the DMN. Here, reactivity takes over. Say you're faced with a challenging social situation like a meeting at work that you know will be loud and dominated by extroverts. Your immediate reaction is tension: you shut down or, if possible, avoid the situation altogether by skipping the meeting. When you skip the meeting, you feel better in the moment, but this reinforces the behavior of skipping the meeting. By removing the unpleasantness, you'll be more likely to skip meetings in the future.

The next level of awareness is *reactive with a mindfulness reset*. Here, you know you are reacting and can bring mindfulness to the situation and make choices about how you will respond. You can think of this as *response* over *reaction*. Go back to the meeting scenario. Say you enter the meeting and feel your mounting physical reactions: tension in your jaw, increased sweating, and butterflies in your stomach. You feel oppressed and overwhelmed. This is the initial reaction and it arises involuntarily. The tension in your jaw becomes a cue to take a mindful breath. You link a few breaths together in awareness. Now that you have brought attention to your body, you start to relax. Your brain's initial reaction was to detect a threat and sound the alarm of a stress response. Now that you have brought awareness to the situation, you recognize it is a false alarm and you sound the "all clear" signal. The tension eases and you find that you are able to engage more in the meeting. More importantly, you stay in the meeting.

The third level of awareness is *responding in the moment.* It occurs when you no longer perceive this meeting, which you had perceived as a threatening situation in the past, as a threat. This level of awareness could be the outcome with committed mindfulness practice.

These levels of reaction were found in a study by Taylor and colleagues (2011). This small study looked at people who had just learned mindfulness (twenty minutes of practice each day for seven days) compared to a group of Zen meditators with one to three thousand hours of practice experience. All the subjects were shown images designed to provoke pleasant, unpleasant, or neutral emotions. Their brains underwent neuroimaging with a functional magnetic resonance imaging (fMRI) machine as they looked at the images. Compared to subjects with no meditation experience, the beginning meditators were significantly more able to turn off an emotional reaction to a negative image. They were able to engage *reactive with* a *mindfulness reset* versus *reactive without awareness* for those without meditation experience. This "reset" skill involves making the amygdala—an important brain structure in the limbic system, or emotional brain—more pliable. The amygdala is a key structure in the stress response. It authorizes the hypothalamus to generate the physiological changes of the stress reaction. The amygdala is often discussed in the context of detecting fear, and this is certainly one of its functions. More broadly, though the amygdala seeks to pay attention to the most important thing in the current (or even imagined future) environment. Mindfulness practice appears to help keep the amygdala from getting stuck in an "on" position. Less reactivity reduces stress. This ability to deactivate the amygdala was not found with the advanced meditators. Instead, they were more skilled at turning off their default mode networks—that is, *responding in the moment*. In other words, there was no story of how awful things were pushing their systems into reactivity. Their amygdalae were less likely to perceive the situation as a threat. In a sense, their threat detection system had been recalibrated, allowing them to live in the world with more ease.

People have been meditating for thousands of years, and now science is starting to confirm what people have observed in their experience over millennia—that meditation changes the way that they experience the world. One thousand hours, the minimum number of hours these advanced subjects practiced meditation, is the equivalent of an hour a day for three years or twenty minutes a day for nine years. When you find yourself getting distracted on the cushion or impatient with the meditation process, you can look forward to these long-term benefits of practice. The world may become a less ominous place where joy can prevail. In the meantime, the data suggest that you can learn to be less reactive in the near term, too.

Mapping Reactivity

Start to pay attention to the situations that make you reactive and document the reactions that you have: physical, emotional, and behavioral. One example is provided for you. Fill in other situations that you have experienced. (Additional copies of the form, if you need them, are available online at http://www.newharbinger.com/36101.)

Reactions to Everyday Situations

Situations that Provoke Reactions	Reactions		
	Physical	Emotional	Behavioral
Meetings at work	Sweating, tension in jaw	Feel overwhelmed, oppressed	Avoid eye contact, avoid meetings whenever possible

Jim's Story: Loving Himself as He Is

Jim is a quiet, thoughtful introvert. He is a real-world example of an awakened introvert. After twenty-five years at the same company, his department was reorganized and he was out of a job. This transition forced him from a comfortable, familiar, and predictable social and work environment to an alien, uncertain, and unstructured pattern of living. Jim describes, in his own words, the biggest introvert challenges in this transition. "Feeling comfortable in my own skin. Loving myself as I am. It takes a lot of energy to form new social connections and to stay engaged with the social connections I already have. Mindfulness practice helps me to have this energy. Given everything that I've been confronting, asking for help has been the biggest challenge."

Mindfulness has opened up a whole new world in Jim's "interior." To this point, he says, "I don't feel as if I was conscious of my interior—physical or mental or spiritual—until I started meditating. It may get me into trouble insofar that it opens up changes in me that cause disruptions to my established habits, patterns, and connections, but it's all for the better. I welcome that kind of trouble. Mindfulness opens up the door to awareness of my interior—an enlightenment—that helps me recognize unhealthy, negative behaviors and thoughts. With that awareness comes the recognition of choices and an opportunity to change. It also helps me recognize my positive, healthy thoughts and behaviors, giving me the opportunity to reinforce and strengthen those patterns. Mindfulness cultivates my equanimity, letting me be at peace with my introversion, lessening the impulse to try to appear extroverted to conform to expectations in social situations."

Attention, Training, and Progress

Attention is perhaps our most precious resource. While all brain functions are critical, most rely on attention for their expression (think of intelligence, creativity, communication, and just about everything else). Yet attention is also the thing that you probably take most for granted. It is so intimate to who you are that you tend to overlook it or to think that it has more capacity than it does (Goleman 2013). Attention is a skill that needs to be trained, practiced, and nurtured like any other, but we're rarely ever shown how to do this. We were all expected to pay attention in school, but almost none of us was shown how.

There is a growing movement called Mind Fitness that teaches mindfulness to active duty military personnel. The movement has adopted the physical fitness metaphor for the mind. Like all metaphors, this one is good at highlighting some aspects of mindfulness and not as good at showing others. We can see the untrained mind as unfit. It is a flabby couch potato, unable to sustain itself for even more than a few seconds until it is off chasing the future and dredging up the past. By practicing mindfulness, you make your capacity for attention more responsive, more fit. And just like exercise, you actually need to do it—that is, you need to meditate and practice being present throughout your day in order to get the benefit. Looking at the weights at the gym can't make you fit; you actually have to move them. Likewise, you have to move your attention from the DMN to the sensations of the present moment to get your mind fit. Where the metaphor breaks down is in the area of progress. If you engage in a physical fitness program, you can chart your progress with reliable predictability. X amount of effort will result in Y amount of results. While you may hit plateaus along the way, progress is linear: effort in, results out. You cannot expect the same predictable results with mindfulness practice. Progress with mindfulness practice follows an upward spiral function as shown in the figure below.

THE SPIRAL FUNCTION
Variability of Progress on the Path

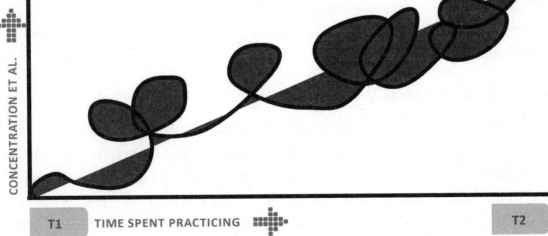

CONCENTRATION ET AL.

T1 TIME SPENT PRACTICING T2

You can plot a line of progress from your starting point of practice to where you are now. This could be seen over weeks, months, or years of practice. In any given moment, the upward slope of that line may be obscured. We are relative creatures, meaning we have the tendency to compare ourselves to recent markers. It doesn't matter if your absolute progress has improved from the beginning; if your relative progress in the near term is down, you'll feel frustrated. If you were at a high point and now have swooped down to a lower point, you may be frustrated about that relative change in position. You've lost sight of the fact that this position is still far ahead of where you started. It can be helpful to step back and try to see the big picture of your mindfulness efforts. Don't put too much emphasis on any given moment's progress or seeming lack thereof. Trust that, over time, you will see the benefits of practice. When you persist with practice, you can expect that your capacity for concentration will increase, practice will be pleasurable, and you will experience states of relaxation. In any given moment, however, you may contend with some intense emotions that have gotten stirred up in the process of life or from your practice itself. Don't overinterpret these difficult episodes as signs that your mind is just too recalcitrant to be trained. Keep practicing, and spend more time returning your attention to the present moment than evaluating the quality of your practice.

Meditation FAQs

Your attitude is much more important that any technical considerations with practice. However, the following details can help to facilitate your meditation experience.

Should my eyes be open or closed?

This is one of the most frequently asked questions. Whatever you are most comfortable with can work. Different teachers and traditions recommend different approaches. Eyes closed can remove one form of distraction, but it also makes it more likely that you will fall asleep. If you practice with your eyes open, you can keep your gaze soft, as if you aren't looking at anything in particular. You can experiment with both eyes open and eyes closed. If you feel sleepy, keep your eyes open. This will help keep you from falling asleep.

What do I do with my hands?

Do whatever is most comfortable with your hands. You can place them palms down on your knees, or palms up. You can clasp them together and rest them in your lap or lay one hand on top of the other. Traditionally, the left hand is placed over the right and the tips of your thumbs can touch (this is known as the cosmic mudra). Whatever you do with your hands, try to keep them relatively still. This will be a unique experience for them; hands rarely stay still.

What should I wear?

You don't have to wear any special clothes to practice. Wear something that is comfortable. It can be a good idea to wear layers; that way, if you're too warm, you can take a layer off.

Do I need to have one of those fancy expensive cushions?

The traditional way to practice meditation is to sit on a cushion (often called a *zafu*) that rests on a padded mat (called a *zabuton*) that sits on the floor. If you sit on the floor, it can be helpful to have one of these cushions. They vary in price and can be filled with either cotton or buckwheat hulls. Some newer ones also contain memory foam. If you are not ready to invest the $50 plus for the *zafu* (the *zabuton* mat adds more expense), you can use bedroom or couch pillows. You can also fold up blankets to serve as a mat. Anything that gets your hips above your knees will do the trick, and this includes sitting in a chair, which does this automatically.

Do I need candles, incense, or bells?

None of these accoutrements is required. It is useful to have a timer of some kind. You can use your smartphone alarm, and there are many apps that you can use, too. Some people find making some kind of altar—with candles, beautiful or meaningful objects, and images—helpful for supporting their practice. The props won't do the practice for you, but they can be a helpful adjunct for some people.

Where should I practice?

It is possible to practice anywhere. That is one of the wonderful advantages of mindfulness practice: it is eminently portable. You can do it in an airport or on a bus. You can do it in your home or at a meditation center. However, it can be helpful to designate one part of your home as your dedicated practice space. Don't do anything other than practice in this spot. Committing precious home real estate communicates your intent to practice, and over time you will come to associate this spot with mindfulness. If you don't have the room available for a dedicated practice area, try to practice in a single spot that you clear away each time you are ready to practice.

Is it okay to fall asleep?

Falling asleep is a very common experience with meditation. When your body becomes still, the tiredness you have been carrying around with you is suddenly apparent. If you are sleepy, this suggests that you are not getting enough sleep at night (see the section on sleep hygiene in chapter 6). Most teachers discourage their students from falling asleep. However, if you think about mindfulness meditation as the practice of paying attention to what is happening now, then feelings of sleepiness can *be* the experience of now. You can investigate these sensations as you would any other physical feeling—and you may even fall asleep! To avoid falling asleep, you can open your eyes or even stand up and practice standing for a few minutes. You can also do walking meditation practice, such as walking slowly, coordinating your steps to the natural process of your breathing—that is, take a step on your in-breath and another step on your out-breath.

What do I do about noise?

Nothing. Noise is part of the landscape of now. The idea that meditation should be done in protected silence is only that—an idea. Since you live in the world, it can be good to meditate in the world and its noises—people talking, cars driving by, air conditioners and refrigerators humming and turning on and off, and countless other things making noises of one kind or another. Try not to exclude any experiences such as noise. If a car alarm goes off while you are watching your breath, you may shift your attention to the car alarm for a few moments to investigate that with interest and then return your attention to breathing when it stops or no longer feels like a novelty.

Should I turn my phone off, or on silent?

Yes! Giving yourself the opportunity to practice is a positive act of self-care. Unless you have a critical emergency, give yourself the time to practice. There are exceptions, of course—your wife is pregnant and the baby may come at any time, a family member is critically ill, you have a job that requires you to be on call, and other situations like these. But remember these are exceptions—give yourself the time to practice regularly without interruption. Also, turn off the ringer on landline telephones and choose a time of day when you are less likely to be interrupted.

What time should I meditate?

Meditation can be valuable at any time of the day. It is largely a matter of personal preference. If you meditate earlier in the day, this will set a mindful tone for your day. If you practice later in the day, this will help you to sift through all the thoughts, emotions, and images of the day. You can also practice in the middle of the day. Try practicing at different times to notice the differences that occur. Aim to practice at the time of day that will make it most likely that you will practice regularly.

How long should I practice?

There is no magic number. The most practical answer to this question is that some practice, of whatever length, is better than no practice at all. Some teachers recommend twenty minutes for practice. If you go to a meditation retreat, the practice times will be longer, often forty-five minutes to an hour. You can punctuate your day with brief practices (see sections on informal practices; these will appear in different chapters) or even do a couple of shorter practices throughout the day. Research suggests that between twenty and forty-five minutes per day over the span of eight weeks can lead to measurable and beneficial changes in your brain.

What if my mind won't stop talking?

This is not a problem. Repeat: this is not a problem. The goal of mindfulness practice is not to quiet your mind. The goal is to notice what your mind does, and one of the things your mind does is talk—a lot! Your job is to keep extricating yourself from whatever your mind talks about, not to extinguish the talk altogether.

How do I handle discomforts?

Uncomfortable sensations are an inevitable part of life and meditation practice. Suppose an itch arises when you are practicing. The natural tendency is to scratch that itch. In fact, you may reach to scratch it without even thinking about it. Similarly, when sensations of discomfort arise from prolonged sitting in the same posture, the reflex tendency is to move your posture to relieve the discomfort. The goal of practice is not to be uncomfortable, but these uncomfortable sensations provide an opportunity for learning, discovery, and change. See if you can greet the itch with awareness: *Oh, there is an itch.* Then investigate the itch with curiosity: *Hmmm, I wonder what this itch* really *feels like.* When you examine it closely with interest, you will discover things that you may not have realized before. An itch, when observed long enough, will change. It may intensify and then diminish. It may come and go in waves. Eventually, it will dissipate. By not *having* to scratch the itch, you have gained a degree of freedom.

How do I handle pain?

Pain is a more intense form of discomfort. The key with painful sensations is to distinguish *hurt* from *harm*. Hurt is like the itch; it is uncomfortable, perhaps intensely so, but no harm will come if the sensations it brings are observed instead of relieved immediately. Harmful sensations contain important information and require action—for example, a change of posture to prevent harm. You have to know your own body to make the distinction between hurt and harm. If your legs fall asleep, this may be a strange sensation but, for the short period of meditation, it will not cause lasting harm. However, if you have a knee injury, sitting in prolonged pain may cause damage. Always put self-care first.

Should I practice with other people?

It can be a benefit to practice with other people. As with exercise, it can help to have a buddy so you can motivate each other to practice. You can also find a place in your community where meditation classes are held. Some of these classes may be offered free of charge. When you sit with others, you tend to sit up straighter and put more energy into your practice. You are much less likely to give up before the end of the session when other people are around. Meditating alone with others around is an ideal scenario for introverts since you don't have to make small talk during practice. Depending on the situation before and after meditation, there may be socializing, but the practice itself is deliciously quiet.

Does mindfulness meditation conflict with my religion?

Mindfulness meditation is not a religion, although it has been associated with the religions of Buddhism. Mindfulness, as often taught in the West, is a secular practice for training the mind. It requires no beliefs, rituals, or affiliations. It is a psychological practice and should be compatible with any religion. In fact, whatever your religious persuasion, mindfulness may actually make you a better Jew, Christian, Muslim, atheist, and so on by helping you to increase your capacity for attention.

Does meditating make me a Buddhist?

No. While the historical Buddha did a practice similar to mindfulness meditation, he was not a *Buddhist,* and nor will you be when you practice mindfulness. Mindfulness is about paying attention, and while it has an ethical component, it transcends any particular religious creed.

Do I need a teacher?

It is not necessary to have a formal teacher, although it can help to have one, especially if you want to deepen your practice. You can find teachers at retreat centers such as the Insight Meditation Society in Barre, Massachusetts, or Spirit Rock in Woodacre, California. The Resources section at the end of this book has more information on practice centers.

What's the next step?

There are many fine books available on practicing mindfulness. See the Resources section for a listing of mindfulness resources, including guided meditation recordings.

Concluding Thoughts

Mindfulness provides a straightforward set of tools to enhance your life. These practices can help you to be more comfortable and less stressed by your incursions into the interior of your mind while also helping you to deal with the stresses that arise from incursions into the extroverted world of commotion. Mindfulness—from formal periods of meditation to bringing greater awareness to everything that you do throughout your day—can become part of your daily life. Every moment can be one of mindfulness or mindlessness. The more you practice, the more likely it is that you will be able to catch yourself when your mind gets caught up in stories about the past or speculations about the future and gently return it to the present moment. The goal of meditation practice is not to log hours on the cushion, but to integrate presence, awareness, and calm into every moment of your life.

These tools will make you a better introvert by honing your time in the interior and expanding your range in the world. Mindfulness can help you to engage your mind in more skillful ways that will bring you more joy, peace, and equanimity—an ability to handle *any* circumstance with calm engagement. Mindfulness can empower you to be more present in your life, to savor your experiences, and to open yourself to what life has to offer. The remaining chapters in this workbook will build on this mindfulness introduction to provide you with a comprehensive set of tools for thriving in the here and now.

Chapter 3

Inviting Quiet into This Noisy Life

S ilence used to be golden, but now it seems to be a rare phenomenon. Quiet, like paradise, may be lost in the frenzied busyness of contemporary life. The hectic pace of life has sped things up and squeezed out the quiet places. The seventeenth-century French philosopher and mathematician Blaise Pascal (1958) said in Pensée 139, "All the unhappiness of men arises from one single fact, that they cannot stay quietly in their chamber." Despite your introvert proclivity for quiet, it can still be difficult to find the quiet repose Pascal recommends. Life has become so busy, so noisy, that you may need encouragement to give yourself permission to be quiet. This chapter is that permission, and will reconnect you to the quiet that is your birthright through inspiration, exercises, and an investigaton of the different types of noise that encroach daily, even moment by moment, in life. Quiet is yours to embrace right here in this moment.

As an introvert, you have an inside route to averting the unhappiness that Pascal points to. You have likely discovered that you require more quiet in your life because you are more sensitive to the stimulation of the everyday world. Quiet provides a respite from the stress of noise and, in many cases, "noise pollution"—noise that becomes noxious, aversive, and stressful. Quiet is a place where you can come to know yourself, restore your energy, and have a more profound connection with the world. As an introvert, you may be naturally drawn to quiet, yet the busyness of everyday life with its ceaseless commotion may impinge on your quiet in ways you may not realize. This chapter will examine different aspects of quiet and ensure that it has its proper, restorative place in your life.

Beloved meditation teacher Ajahn Brahm (2014) tells an endearing story about what just might be an introverted dog that seeks refuge every day at a neighbor's quiet house. He goes inside, curls up in a corner, sleeps for a few hours, and then departs. The dog is well fed and cared for, so the woman who lives alone in this house knows he is not a stray. Finally, her curiosity leads her to write a note to the dog's owners and attach it to his collar, inquiring about the dog's behavior. She gets the following note back: "My dog lives in a noisy house with my nagging wife and four children, two of whom are under five. He comes to your house for some peace and quiet and to catch up on his sleep. May I come, too?"

It turns out the dog's owner is likely an introvert, too!

Where is the quiet in your life? Do you wish that you, too, could curl up at your neighbor's quiet home and catch up on your sleep? Do you have a quiet room where you can sit alone, if only for a few moments? Have unrelenting to-do lists and the noise of twenty-four-hour news and information squeezed quiet out of your life? Has quiet been replaced by text messages, status posts, and voice mails? Perhaps you find bits of quiet at church or at the end of your yoga class, but where else? Think about the quiet spots in your life. Use the space below to write down all the places and times in your day that you experience quiet:

_____

_____

_____

_____

If the space above is overflowing with examples of quiet, you might want to skip to the next chapter. If, however—as will likely be the case—life's noise has intruded and squeezed quiet out, you will have to augment this list to include more places and times in your day and week when you can be free from noisy activity.

How does quiet make you feel? Can you recall a recent time when you found yourself free from human- and machine-made noise and even from the noise of your own mind? How did that feel?

_____

_____

If the quiet felt good, you'll want more of that. If any part of it felt uncomfortable, you may need to reacquaint yourself with the lower kinetic energy of quietness. The exercises in this chapter will help you to reclaim, recast, and re-vision the quiet opportunities in your life. This familiarity will help you to transform what had been potentially uncomfortable into an opportunity for increased self-awareness. If quiet is a comfortable place to be, the exercises will give a new way of inviting quiet into your days.

Quiet can be found in a shift of perception. You can look at objects or the spaces that surround the objects. Quiet is found in that surrounding space. Quiet is also found in the vanishing points in music—the moments of cessation between the notes. The space in between can be just as vital as the content. Inviting quiet into your life suggests expanding these pauses into longer stretches of time. You can create a familiarity—an at-homeness—with space. Quiet is like water. It is not optional, and just as you need to drink half your body weight in ounces every day to stay healthy, you need ample quiet in order to experience balance in your life and to recover from your excursions into extroversion.

Different Kinds of Noise

There is a classic teaching story about a man who escapes the busy city—the noise of people, cars, and the speed of life—for a silent retreat in nature. When he arrives at his woodland retreat, he relaxes into the stillness. Moments later he notices that things aren't as still as he first thought. The wind blows through the trees, making a rustling sound. The brook babbles. Birds sing and insects buzz around. The sounds begin to drive him crazy, and he even attempts to rearrange the rocks in the stream so they won't make so much noise. To avoid the fate of this poor man, you can open yourself to the ambient sounds around you, whether they are natural or human made. As this story reveals, there can be "noise" even in a quiet place when the mind is unsettled. It is also possible to be "quiet" in a noisy place when the mind *is* settled. Both the inner attitude and outer environment are important. It is fortunate when the inner and outer landscapes cooperate in quiet. However, you don't have to rely on fortune; you can train your mind and arrange your life to bring ample doses of quiet into it.

Different kinds of noise interfere with quiet, for there is no such thing as pure quiet in the day-to-day world. What you want is a *relative* quiet. Absolute silence is actually disquieting. When you think about quiet, don't try to exclude the ambient sounds of nature: the birds chirping, the frogs peeping, the crickets conducting their string symphonies. Even background noises that are human made can accompany the quiet that will nurture your introvert predisposition.

Human-Made Noise

If you live in a city, you are exposed relentlessly to the human-made noise of construction, cars, and traffic. If you live in the suburbs, you have neighbors to contend with, and even in the country, where you get respite from some of the city and suburban noises, you get exposed to others like tractors and bleating lambs. Humans are highly adaptable and can get used to just about anything. If you live around constant noise, you may not even consciously notice it any longer. However, noise still affects you at an unconscious level and can elevate stress. Finding quiet places is a greater challenge in the city environment. The best you may be able to do is find places that are relatively quiet. Think about the places near your home or workplace where you might be able to find respite from human-made noise:

_____

_____

_____

_____

The Noise of Talk

Another threat to quiet is the human-made noise of talking. Kahlil Gibran (1969) said of talking, "You talk when you cease to be at peace with your thoughts; and when you can no longer dwell in the solitude of your heart you live in your lips, and sound becomes diversion and a pastime" (60). Think about how often you talk just to fill a space. You probably do this less than your extrovert contemporaries, but even introverts can have a tendency to distract themselves and others with talking. The peace that Gibran talks about is fleeting and elusive and may even be uncomfortable. Think about all the talking you are exposed to every day, including your own and that of others. If you work in an open-plan office, you may be exposed to quite a lot. If you have a lot of extroverts in your life, then talk may be a near-constant feature of your environment. Think about the times during your day that are absent of talking. Write these down:

_____

_____

_____

_____

Human-Made Information

Another type of noise comes from media—human-made information. These intrusions into quiet include social media, the Internet, cable television, and anything that comes through your smartphone, including music. Do you, like most people, spend hours each day engaged with these types of media? Add up the amount of time you typically spend with each medium.

Media Consumption

Media	Daily	Weekly
Internet Radio		
Music		
Podcasts		
Radio		
Social Media		
Television		
Other		

Are you surprised by how much time you spend with these media? If so, setting aside these sources of information is an opportunity to find quiet in your day.

Mind and Body Noise

Now you can turn your attention to "interior" noise.

The mind can be quite busy even if the outer environment is quiet. Reading is a great activity and one that introverts love. The type of noise it creates may be quieter than television noise, but it is still noise in the sense that it is an activity that brings verbal information into the mind. If you love to read, great—keep reading. The invitation here is to find time beyond reading that is at a deeper experience of quiet.

Another category of noise is the busyness of the body. It is likely rare that you are not engaged in a goal-directed activity or working through your to-do list. The day demands action: cleaning, organizing, cooking, driving, working, playing, talking, and planning. Are there times during your day when you are doing nothing? Think about these and write them below:

_____

_____

_____

The undiscovered territory of your own mind is where a lot of commotion takes place. How often is your mind talking, comparing, and wanting to share every experience it has with someone else? Mindfulness practice will help you to discover how busy your mind is and provide tools to help you find some interior quiet. Mindfulness will also help you realize that you can rest your body from its constant activities to relax into the moment.

Look at the table that follows and see where quiet resides in your life as you move through the day from waking to bedtime. Put a check mark in the cell for the places where this type of noise shows up in your day.

Quiet and Noise Throughout Your Day

Activity	Media (music, news, television, radio, smartphone)	Humans (talking, doing things like cooking, cleaning)	Ambient noise (not from the natural world)	Internal landscape busy (thinking, internal self-talk, imagining)
Waking up				
Taking a shower in the morning				
Morning hygiene				
Morning cup of coffee				
Driving to work				
At work				
Driving home				
At home in evenings				
Weekend mornings				
Weekend afternoons				
Weekend evenings				
Other				

If you've gone through the table and you have a lot of check marks, then it might be time to reevaluate the place of noise in your life. If you are not finding enough quiet in your life, where can you bring in more? Each of the cells of this table represents an opportunity to change a habit. Perhaps instead of waking up to the morning news, you can wake up to a melodious tone—something without words—and see how that feels. Instead of planning your day during your morning shower, just pay attention to the experience of taking a shower. A shower provides a wide array of sensory experiences: tactile sensations, temperature, and movement—the sensations of water drops hitting your skin, the warmth or coolness of the water, the steam as you breathe it in. All of these can be attended with interest *and* quiet. Chances are you'll feel better through the rest of your day if you start with an informal mindfulness practice while you shower instead of planning, rumination, and anticipation. Here you try to do nothing. Of course, you are always doing something—moving, sitting, standing, walking—but you can also consider a relative quiet where you aren't caught up in acting on and checking off items on your to-do list. You can extricate yourself from the incessant activity of your storytelling, default-mode-network brain and reengage your attention in the very experience of this moment. You can enjoy a more spacious, relaxed, and patient way of being.

Informal Practice: *Morning Coffee Meditation*

Bring mindfulness and quiet to the process of making and drinking your morning coffee (or beverage of your choice). Find a nice spot in front of a window or on a porch, and sit there with your coffee. Enjoy your coffee alone or with another who has agreed to silence. Attend to your senses. Listen to the trees swaying in the breeze; hear the birds chirping and calling (if you are outside or it is warm enough to open the window). Look at the patterns and shades of green made by the lawn, trees, and foliage. If it's winter, appreciate the muted colors or the white of the snow. Taste the complexity of the coffee. Appreciate the absences: no human voices, no technology, and no to-do list. When your gaze catches something that reminds you of your to-do list, move your gaze back to the natural landscape. Sit and breathe with no particular agenda. If your mind steers into something stressful, reel your attention back to the nature around you or the taste of the coffee and then let the mind reel out again with no particular agenda. If you don't have ready access to nature, you can still look out your window and appreciate the absence of your involvement with the human activity that you observe. Instead of seeing cars, people, and other things, look for the colors, shapes, and movements. Appreciate that you are not involved just yet in the hustle and bustle around you. This is a less formal way of doing nothing than meditation, where you pay attention to breathing and other sensations.

Meditation Reflection

Take a few moments to reflect on what came up for you during this practice. What did you discover? How did the task of focusing impact your experience? How do you feel now?

_____

_____

_____

_____

Three Levels of Activity: Goal Directed, Non-Goal-Directed, and Contemplative

Quiet depends on the quality of the attention you bring to any given moment. You can have restorative quiet on a noisy subway platform if you can bring mindful attention to that experience. Without mindful attention, you may find that you're like the restless man discussed earlier in the chapter who went on a retreat but couldn't find silence; you may find that sitting under the stars in the country with nothing but peepers can be a "noisy" experience of replaying past conversations, anticipating the future, and complaining about the mosquitos. In any given moment, you'll be applying your attention to different types of activities.

Consider three different levels of activity: goal directed, non-goal-directed, and contemplative. Goal-directed activities, as the name implies, aim toward a goal. They can be quiet or noisy. You can do something quietly, like read a book—that's goal directed and it occupies your attention. Driving through rush-hour traffic is also goal directed, and if you listen to the evening news as you drive, your driving time may be quite noisy. You can pay your bills in silence, but this is not an interior quiet task because you are engaged at a pragmatic level and likely have some energy that may be tinged with stimulation (especially as the task is paying your bills). You can have interior quiet vacuuming the house, but the ambient noise will likewise create a level of stimulation that precludes a deeper quiet.

Non-goal-directed activities do not have an explicit goal like goal-directed ones do. Technically, every action has a goal, even meditation, but you can think of activities that are somewhat non-goal-directed, such as napping, being lazy, and browsing. In browsing, there is no intention of buying—just stimulating the senses, without an acquisitive mindset. These are examples of doing *nothing in particular* that can be restful. These relaxed activities can help you to restore energy when it has been depleted by extroverted excursions. If you are constantly busy, both on workdays and on weekends, then you will need periods of quiescence: stillness, tranquillity, peace, and rest.

Finally, there is contemplative activity: here you engage in quiet activity that involves attending to the present-moment experiences of breathing, bodily sensations, or movement. Examples would include meditation, yoga, qigong, tai chi, aikido, and many others, including certain kinds of writing.

For instance, you can be quiet and active with your thoughts channeled into journaling practice. When you journal, you can write in such a way to try to circumnavigate your typical mode of thinking. The author, poet, and writing teacher Natalie Goldberg views journaling as a meditation practice when done with some simple guidelines (see "Formal Practice: Writing Meditation" later in this chapter).

Evelyn Underhill (1911) issued an invitation to contemplative attention when she wrote about "the strange plane of silence which so soon becomes familiar to those who attempt even the lowest activities of the contemplative life, where the self is released from succession, the noises of the world are never heard, and the great adventures of the spirit take place" (314). Contemplative activities are still goal-directed activities but reflective ones. They are different than the activities of cooking dinner, paying bills, and sweeping the floor.

The quality of attention is key. Any of the activities discussed so far can be done with a quiet or a noisy mind (and often a combination of the two). Attention can be with the activity itself or somewhere else. The goal is to bring as much attention to bear on the action of the moment as possible. When attention moves away, your task is to gently guide it back and resume paying attention. Repeat this as many times as is necessary, which will probably be a lot!

Formal Practice: *Writing Meditation*

In her best-selling book, *Writing Down the Bones*, Natalie Goldberg (1986) presents journaling as a contemplative practice, a form of meditation. While writing is typically an internally "noisy" activity, Goldberg's approach to writing can help you to hear what is most important to you. By following the instructions below, you can enter into a meditative state while you write, combining outer silence and the movement of your hand and mind. As you practice, your attention will shift from the default mode network of your brain to a mindful presence. The key is to keep your hand moving at all times; even when you don't know what to say, you write something, even if it is to repeat the same word. Write at a speed so it seems you are discovering the words on the page rather than composing them in your head. By keeping your hand moving, you work around your internal editor (the boss of the default mode network) who wants your writing to make sense, to be polished, edited, and to have proper spelling and syntax. It's the legacy of years of school and a perfectionistic streak that resides in most people. The goal here is to push beyond this surface layer of rules to get to content that is raw, unedited, and unexpected. When you let the words spill out without concern for what they might look like to someone else, you start new conversations with yourself. The writing doesn't have to make sense. You can contradict yourself, you can whine, you can confront strong emotions.

Whatever comes up gets put onto the page. This exercise quiets the brain's default mode of thinking and this is where its value lies. It's not about producing something but rather creating a contemplative space where you can relate to your thoughts in a different way. Instead of your thoughts driving the agenda, you can develop a different perspective on them by attending to them in this meditative way.

Sit down in a comfortable spot free from distractions with a writing implement and something to write on. You can write on loose slips of paper or in a journal that is dedicated to your writing practice. Commit to a period of time, perhaps starting with ten minutes. Set a timer to mark the time. Once you begin writing, don't stop until the timer sounds. Write whatever comes into your mind without censorship. Keep your pages in a safe place to protect their anonymity. (This will help you feel free to say everything that comes into your mind.) You can also destroy the pages after you do the exercise, which will also protect your privacy.

Meditation Reflection

Take a few moments to reflect on what came up for you during this practice. Writing spontaneously like this can reveal surprising things. What did you discover?

_____

_____

_____

_____

_____

_____

_____

Making a Quiet Plan

Now that you've had a chance to see how noisy your days are and to contemplate the spaces for quiet in your life, where can you commit to building more quiet into your life? Where are the places where you could establish or reclaim quiet in your life? Make a list of the activities and practices you are ready to experiment with in the table below. Can these become a commitment? Can you make executive decisions yourself or must you negotiate these times with spouse and kids? If these quiet activities and practices are something you can give to yourself, place a check mark in the "Self-Permission" box. If you need to secure permission or involvement from others, check the "Other Cooperation" box. In the last box, place a check mark if you are ready to commit to this change.

Quiet Commitments

Activity	Self-Permission	Other Cooperation	Ready to Commit

One way to introduce quiet into your life is the practice of meditation. Mindfulness meditation can be thought of as the practice of quiet. When you do mindfulness, you set aside your usual mental habits to try something new—attending to the present moment as it is. Instead of distracting yourself with television, your smartphone, and even your own thoughts, you pay attention to natural things that are happening now—like breathing, bodily sensations, and ambient sounds. When your mind goes back to thinking—when you have imaginary conversations in your mind—you notice that and bring it back to breathing. You may have to repeat this process every few seconds—and that is okay. Remember, mindfulness practice is this back-and-forth movement of attention.

It's hard to let go of these internal conversations. They can be compelling, and you may feel it's quite necessary to pursue them. It might be helpful to remember Pascal's admonition that some good may come from sitting quietly alone. (You'll discover more about being alone in chapter 5, Celebrating Solitude.)

Transformational Quiet

Mindful breathing is softened, slowed, and quiet—effortless and expansive. It can fill the whole body. The body loses its distinctions, the edges soften, and it becomes porous, in open exchange with neighboring atoms—no distinctions, delineations, or demarcations. When the inner murmuring of the mind, with its opinions for and against everything, can be quieted, then you can experience a more profound quiet—quiet that reaches the *silence* that Jesuit priest Anthony de Mello, in his book *Seek God Everywhere*, called the "plane of truth," which means not adding anything to the experience of now—*nothing*. Transformational quiet is beyond pleasure and pain. Even pleasure can have some subtext, commentary, or story—wanting it to last, wanting to share it with someone else, and comparing it to some other experience you have had.

When you remove yourself from the noise, relinquish the actions of busyness, and find some peace within your mind, you enter that "plane of truth." Father de Mello (2010) said this of the importance of silence in *Seek God Everywhere*: "There is only one way for people to confront themselves and that is through silence. All of us need to develop a tolerance for silence, a home to ourselves, a place to touch the wellsprings of life inside of us. There is nothing as valuable as silence. All of us must go back and be in touch with our inner resources" (20).

Have you tasted this experience of deeper quiet, what de Mello calls the "plane of truth"? What were the conditions that gave rise to it? Did it change your view of yourself or the world in which you live?

_____

_____

_____

The words of T. S. Eliot in his *Four Quartets* (1968) resonate with Father de Mello's reflection on silence. It is not just a place of rest; it is the place where you will confront your innermost self. Eliot spoke of the silence that can be found between two waves:

> *Quick now, here now*
>
> *A condition of complete simplicity*
>
> *(Costing not less than everything)... (59)*

Silence can be a welcome resting, returning home from exile in the daily forays into busyness. This is valuable and necessary. However, this silence may cost you everything by asking you to give up preconceived ideas about yourself. This deeper kind of silence is restful. It makes no demands; it has no requirements other than the truth of what is. Silence is whole. Nothing is added and nothing is taken away. Silence is independent of conditions. There is a perfection in things being just so. Silence is a reprieve from assault, demand, and imposition. Silence is a blessed wholeness. Deep quiet is grace in the absence of conditions, actions, and demands.

Have you glimpsed this simplicity? What ideas about yourself do you need to give up to find this perfection, wholeness, and grace?

_____

_____

_____

Again in the *Four Quartets*, T. S. Eliot admonished himself to be patient:

I said to my soul, be still and wait without hope

For hope would be hope for the wrong thing; wait without love

For love would be love of the wrong thing; there is yet faith

But the faith and the love and the hope are all in the waiting.

Wait without thought, for you are not ready for thought:

So the darkness shall be the light, and the stillness the dancing. (28)

For Eliot, waiting was the path to faith and to a transformation powerful enough to change darkness into light. He had the wisdom to be skeptical of his thoughts because they were not ready to be spoken. This is a very introverted wisdom. He knew that faith came in waiting, patience, and awareness. He points to the truth touched in mindfulness meditation practice that there is a world of experience beyond words that we can access when we practice becoming quiet. This experience is beyond the concepts of hope and love and the activity of thinking. Eliot rightly suggests that thinking is superimposed on the more elemental aspects of experience—darkness and light, stillness and movement. Faith arises through patience, self-acceptance, and quiet. You can embrace your introversion with confidence, knowing that all forms of quiet are your refuge.

Concluding Thoughts

After reading and doing the exercises in this chapter, you will be better acquainted with quiet and how much noise there is in your life. You have started to incorporate mindfulness and you have also practiced gaining access to your inner voice through the writing exercise. You can begin to move yourself away from the noisy commotions of daily life to the plane of truth. Quiet, along with silence, is something to embrace, nurture, and proliferate in your life. It is the core refuge for your introvert humanity.

Chapter 4

Navigating the Social and Communication Landscape

As an introvert, you probably, at times, find it challenging to navigate the social and communication landscape. In fact, the social aspects of your life may be where you feel most tested by being an introvert. This is not because you lack social skills, but because you like to express these social skills in selective situations. Unlike most extroverts, you don't want to talk with every stranger you meet, go to every party you're invited to, or say hello to everyone at the parties you do attend. But you do move in and out of social contexts all of the time—at home, at work, in your community—and it's important to refine how you approach these situations in a way that benefits—and protects—you as an introvert. That's what this chapter is about.

This chapter will explore the social and communication landscape and provide you with practical tools for navigating its challenges. After a brief look at some things to keep in mind concerning introverts, extroverts, and the social landscape, we'll look at three practical strategies for dealing with challenging social situations— calculating the pros and cons of a social decision, creating a "personal elevator pitch," and meditating your way through the situation. The balance of the chapter spotlights the challenges of communicating with extroverts and offers suggestions for meeting those challenges.

Introverts, Extroverts, and the Social Landscape: A Few Things to Keep in Mind

As I mentioned before, you (and extroverts, too) move into and out of social contexts all the time, but introverts and extroverts do that with a different frequency and intensity of engagement. It's also important to recognize that introverts have a different rhythm of socializing than extroverts. After interacting with people, the extrovert needs very short periods of rest while you, as an introvert, will likely need longer periods of recovery. You'll need some restorative downtime away from social obligations—a time to enjoy some quiet, solitude, and rest.

In the social arena, introverts and extroverts have different preferences, needs, and values. If you are lucky, you have arranged your work and family life in a way that is consistent with your introvert temperament. However, many introverts must work in extroverted environments, or have important extroverts in their professional, personal, or social lives. If you deal with a large number of extroverts or often find yourself in situations that demand you act in an extroverted manner, you may not only feel stressed out but also physically and emotionally off balance. Learning to more successfully traverse extrovert terrain will help you to better manage your energy and to enjoy the lively presence of the extroverts in your life.

Despite their differences, introverts and extroverts can get along and even learn to appreciate those differences. They can also encourage each other in positive, growth-promoting ways. Extroverts are *not* the enemy. They can help to bring balance into your life (just as you can help bring balance to theirs). Extroverts offer excitement and can break the ice, expose you to new things, and draw you out and into social situations. When needed, they can be good for cover, deflecting attention away from you. The goal is to complement your social appetite with the energies of the extroverts in your life—those who have more hunger for high-impact social interactions—and, at the same time, to avoid falling into the trap of trying to keep up with them or comparing yourself to them. When you are able to accomplish that goal, you'll find that extroverts can sometimes—and maybe even often—bring "happy noise" into your life!

Three Social Survival Strategies (and Some Party Tips)

Let's look now at three strategies or tools that will help you when you find yourself in a challenging social situation. All three—the social decision calculator, the personal elevator pitch, and the party meditation—are practical, flexible, and easy to use. (And as a little bonus after the strategies, I'll share a few party survival tips.)

The Social Decision Calculator: Should I Go or Should I Stay Home?

When you receive a social invitation, you may ask yourself, *Should I go, or should I just stay home?* Either choice brings consequences. You face a dilemma: to go to the event burns "energy capital"; to decline burns "social capital." It can be hard to know which is the right choice, and you may need time to reflect and determine which is right for you. To help you with your choice, use the social decision calculator below. (Additional copies of the calculator are available for download at http://www.newharbinger.com/36101.)

Rate each of the following items on a scale from 1 to 10. Consider how much you agree with the item, and how relevant or important it is to you. Higher numbers indicate greater agreement, relevance, or importance.

_____ 1. Do you have enough energy to do the things you want to do?

_____ 2. How important is this event to significant people in your life (that is, your partner, spouse, boss, children, or others)?

_____ 3. How important is the event to a cause that you deeply value?

_____ 4. Are you interested in having a closer relationship with the host or other people attending the event?

_____ 5. Does the event give you options for leaving when you want or need to?

_____ 6. Will you enjoy this event? What's been your experience with this or similar events in the past?

_____ 7. Will you have time to recover afterward?

Total _____

Calculate your score. If it is in the high 40s, 50s, or 60s, you are probably in good shape for attending this upcoming event. If your score is in the teens, 20s, or 30s, you will need to consider this data more carefully. You may, for example, feel some of these questions are more important than the others, such as the feelings of the host or the importance of the cause. In addition to considerations like that, here are some other questions to contemplate:

When was the last time you pushed yourself?

Was pushing yourself helpful, or did you have regrets?

What did you learn?

What does your intuition tell you?

What does your body tell you?

Sit and meditate on these questions during the days leading up to your decision. You can even journal about them using the form available for download at http://www.newharbinger.com/36101. Your tally from the calculator and your responses to these questions can help you to make your "best guess" decision. And, of course, it is always a guess. If you choose to attend and you enjoy the event, that's great. If you don't enjoy the event, think about why: there will always be something to learn.

Sometimes, however, you can't simply make a decision by yourself because others—your spouse, partner, family—are also invited. What do you do then? If you are negotiating your decision to go with an extroverted partner, for example, your conversation can be empowered by taking your responses from the social decision calculator as well as to the other questions above into consideration. Imagine this exchange:

Introvert:	How important is it to you that I go with you to your office holiday party?
Extrovert:	I'd enjoy your company, but it's not that important.
Introvert:	Would you mind going to that party without me?
Extrovert:	Sure, no problem. Besides, Brad's wife is out of town and I know Tim's wife has her own company party at the same time.
Introvert:	Thanks for that. I had three presentations at work this week and we've been invited to two other parties that same weekend. I won't be up for more than one party in the same weekend. Which one do you prefer that we both attend?
Extrovert:	I think Bob's party is going to be a hoot. They've got this great swing band coming to play and there'll be lots of dancing.
Introvert:	I'd rather go to the one at Kate's because I'll know more people there. If you think it's really important for me to go to Bob's, too, I'll go, but then I'll definitely want to skip that shopping trip with your sister the next day so I can recharge myself. Is that okay?
Extrovert:	I guess that makes sense.
Introvert:	Thanks, for your understanding and support, honey. We've got a deal.
Extrovert:	Deal.

Notice there is no sense of apology in this negotiation. It does, however, express a sense of acknowledging limitations and advocating on one's own behalf.

The Personal Elevator Pitch (PEP)

You've probably heard of the "elevator pitch" in relation to business. You find yourself alone in an elevator with the CEO or some other important person; your pitch is a sixty-second or two-hundred-word summary of your business, product, or service that you can deliver to that person. The personal elevator pitch, or PEP, is similar, except that you can use it when you find yourself in a challenging social situation—suddenly standing alone with someone you don't know, being asked what you do, or trying to make small talk. The good news is that the PEP can be shorter and more succinct than a business elevator pitch—only thirty seconds or about one hundred words. You may want to create one PEP for strangers and another for someone you know but haven't seen in a while. Your PEP can contain biographical information or recent experiences, including books you've read, music you've heard, and movies you've seen. The key is to think about these things ahead of time and prepare your PEP. You may want to write your PEP on a notecard and bring it with you to the event. Your pitch helps you to practice the art of small talk. It may come naturally for extroverts, but you will have to work at it. Here are some samples:

Sample PEP: The Stranger Situation: "What do you do?"

Hi, I'm Sally Brown and I am the owner of a local independent bookstore here in town, Black Dog Books. Perhaps you've heard of it? I am excited about some upcoming events at the store. We have best-selling author James Henry coming to do a reading of his latest murder mystery novel, *You Wouldn't Catch Me Dead Wearing That*. I am also excited that I was recently elected to the board of directors for the New England Independent Booksellers Association (NEIBA). NEIBA has more than three hundred members who represent over two hundred bookstores. As you can see, books are really important to me!

Sample PEP: The Familiar Friend Situation: "What have you been up to lately?"

As you know, Alli is now a year old and Zack is almost three. I've got my hands full with the kids and working from home. Sarah's career has really taken off, and she is traveling more for work. I'm pretty much the only stay-at-home dad in the local library group, and I know more about the varieties of diapers than I care to admit. I never thought fatherhood would be both so challenging and so rewarding. Having the kids so much can drain my energy, so I really look forward to the quiet time of their naps, when I do some meditation and rebuild my energy.

Compose your 100-word (or less) PEP for a situation with strangers:

_____

_____

_____

_____

_____

_____

_____

_____

Compose your 100-word (or less) PEP for a situation with familiar people:

_____

_____

_____

_____

_____

_____

_____

_____

Meditating Through the Party

Let's say you've decided to go to the party, and you've written your PEPs. You still may need a little help with the party itself—hence the party meditation, which is our informal meditation practice for this chapter. You can use this meditation during any actual social situation, not just a party. You can also use it before the party to prepare yourself for what is to come. The party meditation is a real-time meditation that will involve movement, since you won't likely be sitting still at the party, and all of your senses.

Before you go to the party, you might want to do a brief breathing meditation. If you feel going to the party is an obligation you must fulfill, you may not be looking forward to it. Pay attention to your body, becoming aware of the places that are registering the energy of this negative anticipation. By bringing mindfulness to how you feel in the "before-party" space, you can keep your mind from proliferating stories about how "awful" the party may be. Adapt the instructions given below as needed for the party or social event that you attend. There are two options; use one or both, whichever you prefer.

Informal Practice: *Party Meditation*

Option 1: *Bring attention to your body and breath as you travel to the party venue. Ground your attention on your breath or body sensations. If you are going with a partner, let your partner know that you will be silent for a few moments and ask that your silence be respected. When you arrive, open your senses to the event. The party will provide rich data for all of your senses. Really look at the setting, the colors and shapes of the people and their clothes. Stay with what you see and appreciate the perception of color and form without pursuing the "stories" that might crop up (such as* Wow, it seems like everyone is having a great time here. How will I fit in?*). Listen to the myriad sounds. Here again, direct your attention to the cadence, rhythm, and melodies without following the stories, associations, and meanings of the sounds. Take a deep breath and appreciate the aromas that are present. When you bite into some food or taste a drink, give your full attention to that experience. Your body may be a seething cauldron of sensations, and you can bring your attention to these sensations as you sit, walk, and stand. See if you can create a quick map of the sensations that are present without evaluating them as good or bad. Whether you enjoy the party or not, if you go through the entire party just attending to your senses, at the very least you will have done some mindfulness practice.*

Option 2: *You can pretend that you are an anthropologist doing a field study on a foreign culture. This metaphor is not too far off, as you may feel as if the extroverts gathered at the party are an alien culture. Like an anthropologist, you are there with your imaginary clipboard, recording observations in an objective manner, as a scientist would. Embracing the image of the anthropologist connects you to what is going on. Continuing with the metaphor, once you have registered the sensory-perceptual impressions of sight, sound, smell, taste, and touch, you can observe the artifacts and the people of this civilization. Examine the bookshelves, the artwork on the wall, and any other artifacts you can appreciate. Observe the people as they mingle. When you find your mind generating strong opinions about what it sees, try to come back to a more neutral registering of what you see—just the facts without the embellishment of opinion. What you see will include colors, forms, and motion. Focusing on perceptions instead of the stories of strong opinions can help you to feel more at ease in that moment.*

You can do the party meditation after the party as well. It can be helpful for metabolizing the emotional energies that were picked up during the party experience. If you aren't alone, you can request a few minutes of silence to go into formal practice. Investigate your body for residual sensations from the experience. Here again, try to refrain from liking or disliking these sensations and seek to register them as accurately and precisely as possible.

Whatever happens during the course of the evening, making mindfulness practice a part of the festivities will ensure that you will derive some benefit from the experience, even if the party does not meet your expectations or if you do not meet the expectations of others who think you should have had the time of your life.

Meditation Reflection

Take a few moments to reflect on what came up for you during this practice. What new options for handling parties and other unstructured social situations seem possible now? What new perspectives have emerged?

_____

_____

_____

_____

Party Survival Strategies

When it comes to parties, it's not a matter of social skills but social preferences that make the difference between enjoyment and misery. Regaling people in conversation may not be your strong suit in a party situation. However, you can find alternative ways to connect meaningfully in a party situation. Here are a few suggestions:

- Help the host with serving and cleanup.

- Play with the kids and the animals.

- Practice mindfulness.

- Be an "anthropologist," studying the people and the place.

- Scope out quiet places for retreat, as needed.

- Arrange your own transportation so you can leave when you want.

- Grab a book from the bookshelf and read it.

- Give yourself permission to escape, if needed (you might find that just giving yourself permission to leave makes it easier to stay).

- Rehearse small talk before you get to the party. Have a handful of topics ready. Have your personal elevator pitch ready to go.

- Be patient and wait for your opportunity to have a meaningful conversation or two.

If you have an extroverted partner, plan a thorough debriefing of the party experience within a few days of the event. If your partner had a good time, he may assume that you did, too. Make sure you let him know how it went for you. Did you do enough planning and communicating before this event? What can you improve for next time? Perhaps you still need to work on determining when it's time to leave the party. What else can your partner do to support you? What can you do next time to make things go smoother? This debriefing will help with future party attendance planning.

Ryan's Story: Enjoying the Extrovert Circus

Ryan was a good athlete in his youth, and in his thirties he took up golf. At first, he only played once a year at his company's corporate retreat, but then, after his divorce, he started playing regularly. He found solace on the secluded fairways. Getting more serious about his game, he joined a local country club. He also thought this would be good for his business, since he now worked for himself as a freelancer. During his first season, he dutifully went to all of the member events and joined the weekly men's league because "it was a great way to meet other members." More than one hundred men would gather every Tuesday night to play, followed by dinner and drinks afterward. Ryan would leave these events feeling exhausted. He often dreaded going but felt that he "should" go, and so he continued to attend. These Tuesday night gatherings were more bacchanal than dinner. Ryan found himself drinking more than he normally would to cope with the din of noise, the backslapping camaraderie, and the relentless small talk. He dubbed it the "extrovert circus."

Two things changed his relationship to these Olympic-caliber social events. One was that a friend sent him an article about introverts, and he found himself described in its pages. He realized that the problem wasn't a lack of social skills—instead, it was that he was pretending to be an extrovert like the other guys. Around the same time, at the suggestion of his business coach, he also began meditating. Now, when he goes to the extrovert circus, he stays within himself and does not try to emulate the extroverts around him. He gives himself permission to listen more than he talks. He marvels at the way that these men can talk so readily, seamlessly, and energetically with one another. He appreciates that without competing with it. He manages this circus with more skill since he invited mindfulness into his life. He feels like he has more self-awareness. As Ryan puts it, "When it comes time for Tuesday night or any of the other club events, I know that I can say no to the socializing that comes after playing golf. I no longer feel like I have to go. I also know when I've had enough, and I tend to leave earlier than I would in the past. I'm also drinking less. I have always enjoyed people watching and the extrovert circus is a great opportunity to do that. I feel my breathing and just enjoy the show."

Social Media

These days, no discussion of the social landscape is complete without mention of social media. Social media such as Facebook and Twitter present both opportunities and challenges for introverts. Environments like Facebook allow you to engage socially on your own time, and also to engage dynamically whenever you feel like doing so: you can stand back or dive in on your own terms. That communication in these environments is primarily in writing also makes them more appealing to introverts. Still, being on Facebook is socializing of a sort, and you may find that the superficial contacts you have in the virtual world are just as draining as the small talk you experience in the real world. You may not want to post the mundane details of your life, yet you want to stay connected with family and friends. You may feel guilty for consuming social media without participating more directly. Can you give yourself permission to do this without guilt? Introvert self-care applies on Facebook and Twitter just as it does everywhere else.

The sheer number of connections that you have may be stressful. As humans evolved tens of thousands of years ago, they lived in small nomadic bands of hunter-gatherers. They would rarely know more than a hundred people or so. It's no surprise that *Dunbar's number*—a number reflecting our cognitive capacity to keep relationships straight—is 150, about the maximum number of people you would know in your lifetime as a nomadic hunter-gatherer. If you have seven hundred friends on Facebook, you can't possibly know them all and keep all their information straight. It may also be stressful to know more than 150 people, even if they are just virtual friends. Because of this, it's important for you to monitor your online relationships just as you monitor your face-to-face relationships to keep your balance.

Introvert and Extrovert Communication Styles

Now that we've looked at the general landscape of socializing, let's examine the particular challenges of communication. Good communication, whether you are an introvert or an extrovert, requires courage, authenticity, and clarity. It's important, though, to recognize that introverts and extroverts have different communication styles, so it's a mistake to assume that all people communicate in the same way.

Not every introvert and extrovert will show the tendencies noted in the table shown, but this table can be a helpful guide in navigating the social landscape. For example, introverts and extroverts will have a different sense of what qualifies as intimacy, privacy, and connection. The challenge—and opportunity—in communicating with extroverts is to maintain an authentic sense of who you are without feeling compelled to conform to extrovert standards or to apologize for not doing so. Your clear, true, and powerful introvert voice can benefit from understanding the difference between typical introvert and extrovert styles of communication.

Introvert and Extrovert Styles of Communication

Context	Introvert	Extrovert
In the moment	Listens	Speaks
Demeanor	Is calm, quiet, circumspect	Is animated, loud, impulsive
Processing information	Takes extra time to process, integrate, and respond	Is quick-witted, fast-talking, in the moment
Content of conversation	Wants to go deep on one or two topics, exudes thoughtful and quiet energy	Is master of small talk, covers many topics, exudes much energy
Flow of exchange	Prefers to be prompted or asked	Offers information spontaneously
Silence	Is comfortable in silence	May fill up the "awkward silence" with words
Telephone usage	Avoids telephone whenever possible, prefers texting	Has no problem talking on the phone
Writing	May prefer writing over talking in some situations	Wants to talk right away

Before reviewing the conversational styles in the above table, you may not have realized the introvert assets available to you—for example, your tendency to go deep and enjoy moments of silence. In the past, you may have been made to feel that these assets were liabilities. Perhaps you were criticized for communication styles that are natural for you as an introvert. For instance, others may have been frustrated with your taking extra time to respond. Now, you can embrace this practice with the knowledge that it reflects your style and your strength in communication. You don't need to apologize for wanting to go deep. Even though not everyone will want to go there with you, it reflects your authentic style. And when you do find someone who wants and needs to go deep, you'll have a fascinating and stimulating conversation.

Taking Care of Introverts and Extroverts in Conversation

Conversations between introverts and extroverts can be challenging. You each have different styles. You each bring different expectations. Without some proactive attention, conversations can produce a gulf between these styles and expectations. You may feel overwhelmed by the extrovert's rapid-fire, unrelenting speech. The extrovert may feel frustrated by your slower, deliberate way of engaging. To help ease these frustrations and to facilitate better communication, you may want to invite the extrovert intimates in your life to participate in an agreement concerning how you converse. Based on introvert-extrovert styles of communication, you will make concessions to them and they will reciprocate. This give-and-take can make communications go more smoothly.

What to Give to Extroverts

- Be aware of your facial expressions; smile more.

- Telegraph what you are thinking—let your conversation partners know where you are at in this moment. To you, a delay in responding means you are working through something, but your extroverted partners may not know this. Let them know you are thinking about what they said and that you'll get back to them with a response.

- Be more demonstrative: nod your head, move your hands, let your conversation partners know that you are engaged.

- "Color outside the lines": your conversation partners may jump borders between subjects. The extrovert's tendency to be all over the place is an invitation to be patient with and mindful of the extroverts you talk to. This is an opportunity to let go of your typical response habits, such as being annoyed, frustrated, or judgmental. (This effort is consistent with mindfulness practice!)

What Extroverts Can Give in Return

- Breathe and try to be patient.

- Recognize that your introvert conversation partners take longer to process information and respond, perhaps longer than you expect or want.

- Pay attention to your breathing during any pauses—and, of course, refrain from talking. Don't jump in and fill in any silences that may emerge during the conversation. Your enthusiasm, though appreciated, can interrupt the introvert thought process.

- Be aware that your ability and tendency to jump from topic to topic is stressful for your introvert conversation partners, so try to stay focused on the point at hand.

- Pay attention to yourself during the conversation—that is, don't let enthusiasm carry you away and your introvert partners along with it. Take your enthusiasm down a notch when speaking with introvert partners.

- Think ahead about requests you might make or decisions you might want your conversation partners to make, because introverts generally don't like surprises. Give your introvert conversation partners time to think about their responses; they don't want to make decisions or be forced to respond on the spot.

- If you do make an impromptu request, don't pressure your introvert partners for an immediate response. Doing so is stressful for introverts.

As you discuss these aspects of introvert-extrovert conversation with your extrovert intimates, promise that you'll reciprocate by following the advice in the introvert's part of this exercise. Together you can enhance and strengthen not only your conversations but also your relationships.

Informal Practice: *Extrovert Fascination Exercise*

The ultimate introvert coping skill is to become fascinated with the extrovert. If you can bring *interest* to your perception, it will replace aversion. You can treat the extroverts in your life with awe, curiosity, and even a bit of envy—"How do they do that!"

So, how *do* you do that in a mindful way? Before I answer that question directly, let me tell you about the classic introduction to mindfulness meditation—the raisin meditation. This practice was introduced by Jon Kabat-Zinn (1990) during the first mindfulness-based stress reduction (MBSR) course in 1979 at the University of Massachusetts Medical Center. The exercise is simple: Take a single raisin and give it your full attention with all of your senses as you eat it. Before you put it in your mouth, examine it with your eyes, appreciating its color and form. Notice how it feels in your hand and in your fingers. Take in its aroma. After investigating the raisin with your eyes, nose, and sense of touch, place it in your mouth and explore tactile sensations and the onrush of taste with your tongue. Finally, bite into it once to explore the sensations of taste further. Taking account of all of your senses slows down the process of eating the raisin. The attitude to take toward the raisin is that of encountering something new. Regard this raisin as if you have never seen a raisin before, as if it is something completely new. Of course, you have never seen this particular raisin before, so the experience *is* new.

Now, can you bring the same sense of reverence to the extroverts in your life? This reverence does not compel you to act like an extrovert but rather to appreciate what it's like to be in the world in the way that extroverts are in the world. *Extrovert fascination* comes from a safe distance of observation—appreciating without needing to compare, needing to keep up, or stressing out. While you observe the extroverts in your world, you can learn something, too. Perhaps it's a lesson on the art of small talk, the use of body language, or how extroverts project their voices in social situations. These observations might have some value for you, not in trying to be like an extrovert but in being an introvert with a greater range of options.

Meditation Reflection

Take a few moments to reflect on what came up for you during this practice. What do you now appreciate about extroverts that you didn't before? What aspect of extroversion appeals to you most?

_____

_____

_____

_____

The Art of Being Light

Not every conversation reflects the deeper issues of life. While you may want to jump right into the meaty part of conversation, most people—and especially extroverts—will need a warm-up period. It's like deep-sea diving: divers can't just go straight down or they will explode. You must descend gradually and acclimate people to the depths you are exploring in thought and conversation. If you are like most introverts, you find making small talk an onerous affair. Extroverts tend to be blessed with the gift of gab, easily engaging in conversations on any topic. Your mind may just draw a blank in such situations. Your tendency is to go for the meaty parts of a conversation because this is where you feel most at home. However, jumping right into the deep stuff can intimidate conversational partners—especially extroverts, but probably many introverts as well. So, you need to learn the art of being light and the skill of timing the shifts in your conversations. In the art of being light, instead of thinking of chitchat as some laborious distraction, view it as a warm-up for the juicier parts of the conversation to come. Just as with exercise, it makes sense to engage in a low-intensity action before moving on to a high-intensity action. It may require some patience on your part to wait for the good stuff to happen. It may also help not to see the concession to small talk as a diversion from what is important to you. Again, there is an art to being light, and this art can be a useful tool in your introvert tool kit.

Monitoring Conversations: A Way to Cultivate Relationships

In navigating the communication landscape, you'll find that conversations range from the superficial to the deeper issues of life. It can be helpful to envision the different types of conversations as a pie chart (see the figure that follows). Consider four types of conversations: strategic, topical-informational, intimate-vulnerable, and complaint. Strategic conversations involve topics such as these: *Who is picking up the kids where? How much should we spend on a new refrigerator?* Topical-informational conversations reflect the flow of the day: *How was your day? Did you hear about this event in the news?* Heart-to-heart conversations require one or both conversation partners to be vulnerable, revealing what is most important to them, so intimate-vulnerable conversations deal with fears, dreams, and feelings (anything that is not strategic or informational-topical). Vulnerable-intimate conversations come from the heart—that is, they resonate with feeling. They are not rehearsed, canned, or contrived. They are a deep, accurate, and meaningful reflection of who you are in this moment. Vulnerable-intimate conversations touch on themes such as *I am feeling uncertain about..., I need to confess..., It would be great if we could talk about this idea that I have for...* It might, at times, be difficult to distinguish a complaint, the fourth category of conversation, from an intimate-vulnerable conversation. Here, you may reveal something important about yourself, but it is presented in a kvetchy, complaining manner: *I can't stand Michael at work.*

He is unreliable, lazy, and divisive. This is a complaint because, other than acknowledging your annoyance, it doesn't reveal much about you. Compare that complaint to this statement: *When I encounter people like Richard at work, I am not sure how to handle it. I don't know whether to confront him or speak to his supervisor. I feel very unsettled when I observe him not doing his share of work.* This statement is an example of an "I" statement. It reveals how you feel in the moment and reflects the dilemma you face at work. If you share this statement with your conversation partner, it could be considered an intimate-vulnerable conversation.

Conversation Types

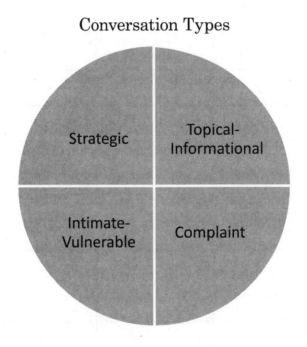

Observe your communication patterns for the next week. Using the following "Conversation Monitoring" table (additional copies of which are available for download at http://www.newharbinger.com/36101), monitor your conversations and place a check mark in the box that corresponds with the type of conversation you had. Tally the results at the bottom.

Conversation Monitoring

Conversation Time and Partner	Intimate-Vulnerable	Strategic	Complaint	Topical-Informational
Totals				

After completing this table, review the results. Which type of conversation predominates? Are you satisfied with the way these conversations are distributed? How would you like to change the pattern moving forward? Are you spending your conversation time in a way that is consistent with your values? What do you need to work on? Are you surprised how much time you spend in strategic conversations or complaints? Write your observations on the lines that follow.

_____

_____

_____

_____

You might want to prepare one table for conversations with your partner or spouse and another for conversations with a good friend or family member, perhaps an introvert with whom you feel comfortable being yourself and always have good, satisfying, and deep conversations. Compare the two tables. This comparison can show you two things. First, it reveals areas that may need work in your primary relationship. Next, it can also reveal the value of surrogates. It may not be possible or advisable to get everything from your partner. And while the work you do with your conversations should help you to improve them to some degree, it may not be possible to get every type. If you find that you don't get enough of the types of conversations you want from your spouse or partner, you may want to cultivate your relationships with other conversation partners for more balance in your life.

Concluding Thoughts

As an introvert, you bring your own style to relationships. You have a lot to offer with your conversation assets; and, with the mindfulness skills you have learned in this chapter, you can be even more present, attentive, and responsive when you are with others. This will lead to a greater sense of connection and thereby satisfaction. The social landscape presents many opportunities for growth, and, here again, your mindfulness practices will help you to stay engaged without getting overwhelmed. After all this socializing, though, you might enjoy a little solitude—the subject of the next chapter.

Chapter 5

Celebrating Solitude

In this chapter, we will celebrate solitude by exploring its power and promise in your life as an introvert. We will also look at some of the pitfalls of solitude in your own life and in your relationships with others, including the challenge of giving yourself permission to seek solitude without guilt. To thrive as an introvert, you need solitude skills. While the desire for solitude may come naturally, the skill of securing it often needs to be practiced. I will provide both practical suggestions and mindfulness exercises that will teach you how to build solitude into your busy life and how to cultivate a "portable" solitude, courtesy of mindfulness. Mindfulness practice helps you to create a supportive context for living in the world as an introvert and, as such, it supports the skills that enable you to establish, maintain, and celebrate solitude in your life.

Before we go any further, I want to explain what I mean by "solitude" in the life of the awakened introvert, because I'm using that term in a bit broader—or deeper—sense than the usual understanding of solitude as being alone. Solitude does not even necessarily require being alone, although it is usually facilitated by keeping company with yourself. Solitude is not lonely either. It is a choice to spend time alone with yourself, often a gift to yourself to recharge your introvert batteries. Solitude invites you to look within, to reconnect with your sense of quiet, values, and intentions. Most importantly, solitude is a state that is self-contained. You don't need anything from anyone else, and no one makes demands on you. As you can see, you could be alone and not feel self-contained; you could feel restless, agitated, or bored.

You could also be together with someone who nurtures your solitude by not being intrusive and not needing you to take care of him or her. This broader and deeper view of solitude creates a natural fit for mindfulness practices that can nurture your solitude further.

Inviting mindfulness further into your life provides a way to bridge the gap between personal solitude and peopled existence. On the one hand, mindfulness can help you to enjoy the solitariness of solitude without feeling lonely. On the other, it can also occur in the context of social connections and what might be understood—and enjoyed—as being "alone in the presence of others" (Salmon and Matarese 2014, 338). This is the approach that the Buddha promoted twenty-five hundred years ago when he gathered people together to meditate in silence. Solitude without social connections would be a form of exile. So, as we look at solitude in this chapter, let's first explore solitude in our lives alone, and then move on to look at solitude in our relationships with others—both those with whom we are intimate and those in our larger social circles. Throughout the chapter, we'll look at ways to enhance solitude in our lives.

Finding Yourself: Embracing the Power and Promise of Solitude

As an introvert, it is crucial that you have protected time during which you can dwell undisturbed in your introvert nature and recharge your energy from excursions into the extrovert circus. Like quiet, solitude provides an indispensable period of restoration for your introvert energy. Solitude *is* a form of quiet where you can be invisible or inaccessible to the demands, needs, and expectations of others. Solitude can also be an interior affair where you are secluded from thinking. With the help of mindfulness, you can have a respite from the incessant activity of your mind—as well as that of the world around you. Salmon and Matarese (2014) point out that it is not noise or stimulation that impair solitude, it is feeling that you *must* do something. You can appreciate solitude in the midst of a loud environment or you can find it elusive in a remote cabin in the woods. But when it occurs, solitude is always found in the present moment—and in that moment, you find yourself.

In his essay "Self-Reliance," Ralph Waldo Emerson wrote, "There are voices which we hear in solitude, but they grow faint and inaudible as we enter the world" (Emerson 1993, 21). Solitude is an opportunity for discovering these voices: *What do I really think about things? Who am I? What do I want?* The answers to these questions may only arise in solitude. It is difficult, if not impossible, to hear your internal wisdom if the outer (and inner) world is noisy. Solitude is the place where you will find yourself. What you discover may be a surprise—and it is always a learning experience. Seek to uncover the vibrancy in the quiet reaches that solitude embodies.

But where can you find solitude in your noisy, overscheduled world? Introvert blogger and author Michaela Chung (2013) provides encouraging insights on finding solitude both within and around us: "Introverts recognize that many of life's greatest moments happen when we are alone. Aliveness seizes us as we are turning over a great idea in our mind. It reverberates through us as we silently soak in a majestic sunrise. On a twilight jog, it is inhaled with each quickened breath... We know that aliveness springs forth from the core of our being and dissipates in solitude, in silence. We do not require a list of adrenaline-inducing activities to feel alive. We need only ourselves" (48).

There is something sacred about spending time alone. The poet Rainer Maria Rilke in his *Book of Hours* (Barrows 2005) recognized this when he said, "I am too alone in this world, and yet not alone enough to consecrate every hour" (67). Rilke's words reflect the definition of solitude offered earlier in this chapter. His aloneness does not in itself guarantee solitude. To experience solitude requires an ability to pay attention to what is happening. It is hard, perhaps impossible, to reveal your true wanting in the peopled clamor of everyday life. In solitude, you may have an opportunity to hear yourself think and to discover what it is you truly want in this world. Without such solitude, it is hard to treat each moment with the reverence that can only come through a full attention to the experience at hand.

Mindfulness as Inner Solitude

Outer solitude is crucial, and without it, you may not be able to develop your inner solitude. Inner solitude is the ability to have a quiet mind. This quiet may only come in moments, but with practice, those moments will come more frequently. While it is appealing to imagine a mind completely free of thoughts, images, and emotions, the reality looks different. It is an idealization to see the mind in meditation as a blank one from which nothing arises. Instead, for both beginners and experienced practitioners alike, interior solitude is a staccato, variegated, or intermittent phenomenon. Attention moves in and out of the present moment. Mindfulness training gives you the skill base to move your mind from noise to quiet. Each time you retrieve your attention from the tantalizing pull of future, past, or commentaries on the present, you create a moment of solitude in your mind. Your attention is protected from the intrusion of thinking. In this case, it is your own thoughts that you seek relief from, instead of the words or presence of others.

The Frequency of Unpeopled Existence: Your Experience with Solitude

Look back over your life for the past few weeks. How many times were you in your own company? How much time did you spend alone? How did it feel to be by yourself in these situations?

_____

_____

_____

Where can you introduce experiences of solitude into your daily life?

_____

_____

The Rhythm of Solitude

There is a rhythm to solitude. It is not unremitting, but instead it goes in and out of being with others. While you may not find it practical to experience complete solitude, you can seek out experiences of "relative solitude" in your everyday activities: Visit an art gallery by yourself. Go to the movies by yourself. For a challenge, and one you may already be quite familiar with, go out to a restaurant to eat by yourself. You are likely to be greeted by the hostess with the inquiry, "Just one?" What's wrong with just one? Proclaim with pride, "Yes, just one." Relative solitude gives you a respite from chitchat, conversation, and that sense of being "on" when you are around other people. You can rest into the silence found in the spaces vacated by others. You can also go for a walk by yourself. Walking provides a way of being with yourself whether you're in others' company or not. It's a self-contained way of moving through the world.

Formal and Informal Practice: *Walking Meditation*

Informal walking practice is a bona fide antidote to the familiar lament, "I don't have time to meditate." You *are* walking in your world every day and you can use this time to practice. As long as you can make the effort to set aside the activity of your default mode network (again and again and again), you can accumulate quite a bit of practice each day. These small sips are different from a longer sitting, but they are nonetheless valuable. Informal walking practice can occur literally any time that you are walking, whether for exercise or just ambulating between point A and point B. You are supposed to walk 10,000 steps each day to stay fit, so why not make as many of these as you can mindful ones?

To make walking an informal meditation practice, just walk as you would normally walk. The difference is that you will also redirect your attention from your internal dialogue to your actual experience of walking.

Formal walking practice is like formal sitting practice inasmuch as you devote yourself to the practice and nothing else. Formal walking practice will be a slower, more deliberate way of walking; you will experience life from the perspective of the body in motion. To do formal walking meditation, you don't need a lot of room. You can stake out a tract of floor and walk back and forth. You can choose a circle or square to follow. I often use an 8- by 10-foot rug that has lots of symmetrical squares—these squares are ready-made rows for walking; I'll also walk around the edge or perimeter of this rug. Any space can do. The eyes are typically left open for walking practice. You can keep your gaze soft, as if you are looking through the things you see rather than right at them. You can do whatever feels most comfortable with your hands. You can leave them free at your sides or fold them in front of or behind you.

The basic method for formal walking meditation is to coordinate your steps to your breathing. When you take an in-breath, take a step with one foot. When you exhale, step with your other foot. The speed of your walking will be determined by the speed of your breathing. Make sure that you don't reverse this—that is, don't let your walking alter the speed of your breathing. When you walk in this way, you can maintain a reasonable pace—one that won't attract too much attention if you are doing this practice in a public place like a train station.

You can slow the process down even further. (If you're doing this in a public place, any of the slower practices will definitely attract attention to you, so be forewarned!) As you inhale, lift your heel off the ground. As you exhale, move your foot forward, and as you inhale again, place your foot down and raise up your other heel. You can also uncouple your breath from your steps and just walk as slowly as you can.

When you do slow walking, you may notice that your balance is temporarily affected. This happens because you change the cadence of your steps and also because you bring deliberate attention to something that is usually automatic. This self-consciousness typically resolves itself, but if you need the support of a wall or if you need to pause and stand to regain your balance, you can do so whenever needed.

Mindful walking is a moving sanctuary; you can enter it whenever you have a few free moments, or it can be your extended daily practice. In combination with informal walking, you can access this refuge many times each day.

Meditation Reflection

Take a few moments to reflect on what came up for you during this practice. How do you see the world differently now that you have walked through it with mindfulness? How do you feel differently now that you have moved through the world in this way?

_____

_____

_____

_____

Being Alone Together: Solitude and Your Intimate Other

Solitude can be practiced alone and with another person. Rilke (2006), in Ulrich Baer's beautiful translation, recognized the value of relationships to support the need for solitude. In one of his voluminous letters written to friends, colleagues, and patrons, Rilke wrote:

> In marriage, the point is not to achieve a rapid union by tearing down and toppling all boundaries. Rather, in a good marriage each person appoints the other guardian of his solitude and thus shows him the greatest faith he can bestow. The *being together* of two human beings is an impossibility; where it nonetheless seems to be present it is a limitation, a mutual agreement that robs one or both parts of their fullest freedom and development. Yet once it is recognized that even among the *closest* people there remain infinite distances, a wonderful coexistence can develop once they succeed in loving the vastness between them that affords them the possibility of seeing each other in their full gestalt before a vast sky! (36, Rilke's emphasis)

Rilke's insights here are profound and germane to introverts. In order to be whole, you must recognize the limitations of human connection. Connections are important yet cannot provide everything that you need. You must give some of this sustenance to yourself. Mindfulness can be thought of as a form of self-relationship that is aware, nurturing, and adaptive. When those closest to you respect your need for privacy, they can serve as guardians of your solitude. If you are lucky, your partner will naturally be your guardian. If this is not happening exactly as you need, you may find it helpful to share this Rilke passage with your partner. These words can also help to facilitate a solitude contract, which can encourage and protect the role of solitude in your relationship. (See "The Solitude Contract" later in this chapter.)

Rilke points to our culture's misapprehension of togetherness. People cannot merge together, even though they are encouraged to (just listen to popular music or watch the portrayals of relationships in movies). People seek their "soul mate," the person who will complete them; Rilke attests that such completion is a myth. As an introvert, you may be better equipped to navigate this solitary territory, since it is in solitude where you find solace, restoration, and silence. Yet as a human being, you also value connection. Finding the right mix of togetherness and aloneness is a delicate balancing act.

Child psychoanalyst D. W. Winnicott knew the importance of solitude. As Winnicott scholar Jan Abram (2010) notes, "The capacity to be alone is based on the paradox of being alone in the presence of another and signifies health and the ultimate of maturity" (41). To be alone together is to enjoy a context of connection. In that mutuality, you can hear your own thoughts, feel your own feelings, and come to know yourself better. In a relationship, each partner recognizes the limits of togetherness: *We can be together, but I can't have your thoughts, dreams, and visions.* Each partner respects the other's autonomy. Each partner commits, to paraphrase Paul in the book of Philippians, to work on his or her own salvation. The commitment to solitude brings an existential authenticity to a relationship and the lives of the partners in that relationship. In other words, there is the opportunity to be real with one another on the level of existence—for instance, living in the present and taking responsibility for one's actions and happiness. In this context of autonomy and solitude, there is freedom to be oneself and to have a mutual give-and-take that serves the growth of one another. It is a mature, grounded way of being in the world.

Solitude as Seclusion

It is possible to be with another and to have solitude if this other guards your solitude. But as an introvert, you may be more sensitive to the energies of the people around you. Just having another person in your space, even if you are not interacting with this person, can deprive you of needed solitude if this person is "loud" in words, needs, and actions. Sometimes you just need to be secluded, alone with yourself.

Do you have a solitude zone in your home? A man cave, or the female equivalent? A meditation space can serve double duty as a place for practice and, by default, a place to enjoy solitude. You may be fortunate enough to devote an entire room to meditation and perhaps yoga. If not, can you find a corner, portion, or section of your house to designate as your solitude space? Even when your partner is the guardian of your solitude, at times you'll need a protected space just to yourself. And if you don't get that solitude from your partner, you'll need this space all the more.

Finding Solitude in the World Around You

The key component to navigating the social milieu is to have adequate solitude in your life. Thoreau advocated the need for solitude when he said, "A man thinking or working is always alone, let him be where he will. Solitude is not measured by the miles of space that intervene between a man and his fellows" (Thoreau 2004, 135). Following Thoreau's wisdom, I am reminded of the times when I seek solitude amid the humanity around me instead of seeking a secluded solitude in nature or on a meditation retreat.

My Story: Solitude Among Multitudes

I am sitting in the café at the Kripalu Center for Yoga and Health in Stockbridge, Massachusetts. I am taking a break from the workshop I am teaching. I am wearing headphones (listening to Pink Floyd, I confess) and writing these words. The laptop and the headphones provide a mantle of invisibility like Harry Potter's magic cloak. The laptop is the introvert's ninja tool—it provides a protective, stealth cover because people are less likely to bother you. Books work, too. Writing can be a solitary lifestyle and often I am home in my office writing alone. Well, to be fair, not completely alone, since I have my dogs and cat with me. But I have solitude from human company. Sometimes this solitude is welcome, and at other times, I want to be around other human beings but not be bothered by them.

When I get that hankering to connect, I'll grab my MacBook Air and head to one of the cafés, restaurants, or bars where I like to write. My portable solitude doesn't require ambient silence. Whether it's music, conversations, or commotion, the noise around me isn't an issue when I bring my mindfulness skills to bear. To be mindful, I don't need conditions to be perfect. When I can include all the action in the landscape of now, I am at peace. However, if I start to exclude any part of that experience, I am bound to get tense, frustrated, and annoyed. Sometimes I will groove on the house music and begin to write. Other times, I may elect to provide my own music, donning headphones and creating a seal of portable solitude. I am still situated in the context of the café and mindful of all its energies—with the skillful addition of my own music, to which I am also attending mindfully.

For me, solitude is not just being alone in the wilderness. The key to solitude is to be in a place where no one makes energetic demands on me. I am left alone to do what I like. I find that I am often more productive in these portable solitude excursions than I am in the quiet seclusion of my home environment. Being in solitude among the multitudes is the ideal environment for my introvert temperament. I feel connected, unencumbered, and focused.

Formal Practice: *Portable Solitude Meditation*

Mindfulness practice provides instant solitude. Basic mindfulness practices such as breathing and body scan meditations are the embodiment of solitude. Wherever you are, even in a crowded subway car, you can create an interior space where you can touch peace, recharge your batteries, and find joy.

Your individual experience, while connected to everything else around you, serves as the foundation for your life. From this foundation, everything else builds—your relationships, projects, and way of being in the world. Attending to your foundation is not selfish, although it is self-oriented. You can think of it as self-fullness rather than selfishness. Being good, peaceful, and helpful starts from the actions and inactions of individuals. If you don't take good care of yourself, you won't be able to be an effective agent for change and goodness in the world. Regular mindfulness practice is a powerful way to take care of yourself. Sometimes, though, you may need an extra boost of mindfulness as you move through difficult situations in the world. This is where the portable solitude practice comes in handy. You can use this one or create your own to use anytime you need an infusion of solitude.

Take a moment to connect with your breathing and do a quick body scan, making contact with the body from the top of your head to the tips of your toes. Allow your attention to sink into your body, resting there. Feel the edges of your breath expanding into your body. It is hard to tell where the breath ends and the rest of the body begins. Feel your breath filling your entire head, neck, and torso. Feel how your arms and legs participate in breathing as your blood flows and carries oxygen. Take a moment to reflect on all the people you are connected to. Notice the feelings that arise as you contemplate your relationships—what you give and receive, and what you want from the people you care for and are involved with. Breathe into these feelings. Now let those feelings and thoughts go and just sit with your body for a few moments. You remain connected to everyone, even when you turn your attention within. If you are in the vicinity of people, whether familiar or strangers, take note of that connection. All the people around you aspire to be happy, just as you do, although they may be caught in anguish, misery, or stress in this moment. Acknowledge your common humanity; then turn your attention within, letting go, for the moment, of your attention toward others. Take this time to nurture yourself. Explore your interior landscape for whatever features are present now. Imagine that you are enveloped in a benign energy. This energy insulates you from strife, noise, and the demands of others. You can rest here and restore your energy. Sounds are present, but you don't need complete silence to foster your solitude. As long as your gaze reflects to your interior, you can sit and move with solitude.

As you dwell in the moment, feel this surrounding energy thickening, providing a dense layer of cover. Here, no one can find you. You are invisible, hidden, and protected. This place is always available inside you. You are not isolated; you are connected with others. You enjoy this cover when you set these connections aside for a few moments in order to rejuvenate your energies in seclusion. Stay here for as long as you can. Come back often.

Meditation Reflection

Take a few moments to reflect on what you discovered during this practice. Has your sense of place within humanity changed? How do you see this new way of relating to energy benefiting you in the days to come?

_____

_____

_____

_____

_____

Solitude and Social Media

Not that many years ago, you could also enjoy technological solitude, but this is no longer possible. It seems almost inconceivable—and now even selfish—that you would want some privacy, quiet, and refuge from immediate connection. Can you remember what it used to be like before smartphones—before you could reach into your back pocket, pull out your phone, and instantly communicate with others in the flash of fingers required to write a text? And if you receive a text, you'd better respond soon, lest your friend thinks you fell off the face of the planet.

Do you feel pressure to maintain larger social networks of "friends" who expect you to connect, and may drop you as a friend if you don't? Worse yet, do you feel harassed by the "read receipt" feature for text messaging? If you read a text and don't respond right away, perhaps because you want to think about it or you are doing something else, your text sender may project all kinds of negative interpretations on you, maybe even taking it as a personal insult that you don't reply instantaneously. The texter may think you are aloof, conceited, or hateful. Suggestion: don't turn on read receipts!

The advantage of social media is that it allows you to participate on your own schedule. If you are not careful, as with the read receipts just discussed, you can get drawn into taxing interactions online just as in person. Social media participation also requires setting limits on others' expectations of how you will participate. You'll need to assess your own energy whenever you decide to partake. Even though it doesn't involve talking, posting to Facebook or tweeting requires energy, and to engage is to give up your solitude in the moment. When you decide to enter the electronic fray, try to bring your mindfulness skills with you. You can take a mindful breath before you jump in. You can monitor your breathing and bodily sensations as you participate and slow things down if you notice that you are moving into a place that you'd rather not be in. You can take a few mindful breaths after participating to clear space for whatever comes next.

Building Your Solitude Skills

We've looked at solitude in your life alone, together with an intimate other, and in the world at large. As you know, the extrovert-dominated culture tends to confuse solitude with loneliness: "Why would you want to spend that much time alone?" Our culture mistakes being alone with being lonely. After all, one is *supposed* to be the loneliest number. This is an unfortunate confusion. Being alone is seen as pathetic. It is something to pity and avoid at all costs. It is as if people are phobic about being alone, and after a lifetime of trying to avoid solitude or being told that it's aberrant, it might be hard to embrace solitude in a positive light. Thoreau in *Walden* echoed a similar sentiment when he observed, "I never found the companion that was so companionable as solitude. We are for the most part more lonely when we go abroad among men than when we stay in our chambers" (Thoreau 2004, 131). You can be lonelier in a crowd than you are keeping your own company. Thoreau favors the quality over the quantity of social contacts and places value on the company kept with oneself. Solitude can be your foundation for reaching out to the world, and without enough solitude in your life, you may feel out of balance, depleted, and lost. To keep your solitude foundation, in this culture that rarely values it, let's look at some attitudes and skills that will help you wholeheartedly embrace solitude.

Caring for Yourself: Solitude Without Guilt and Shame

Do you feel free to claim solitude in your life? Since our culture does not support the idea of solitude (unless you are a rugged individualist, like a cowboy living in the untamed West), you may encounter a lot of resistance to your needs and desires for alone time. People may coerce you to come out of your shell or guilt-trip you to not be "so selfish." Laurie Helgoe (2013) laments, "We have a verb for interacting with people—socializing—but have no single, affirmative verb to describe being alone" (23). *Isolating* is perhaps the best available word, but it has a negative connotation. You could also say "sequestering," "removing," "segregating," or "quarantining," but none of these capture it either. Without a single word to use, you have to work harder to get people to understand. You may find it helpful to redirect the conversation from your alleged selfish motives to your need for self-care. Instead of that one word, you'll need phrases such as "solitude is important to me" or "alone time is crucial for my self-care." Think of some other phrases that you can use to communicate with the extroverts in your life:

_____

_____

_____

You may feel that you need solitude like fish need water. Your desire for solitude is natural, and while it may seem to be a luxury to have it, for introverts it is a necessity. If you don't take care of your introvert needs such as solitude, you will be a less companionable partner when you do engage with others—both the introverts and extroverts in your life.

Below is a list of thoughts about solitude for you to contemplate. They can help you to embrace solitude without guilt and, more importantly, without shame. Shame speaks to a sense of deficiency. There is nothing wrong with you if you desire to be alone at times, even frequently.

- The yearning for solitude doesn't make you a misanthrope or even a loner.

- Solitude is a fundamental human need.

- Solitude doesn't mean disconnection from others.

- Solitude is necessary for you to replenish your energy.

- You have a right to request solitude.

The Solitude Contract

This section will guide you in writing a solitude contract. If you are in a relationship, you can direct this to your partner. Let her know what you need, why it is important, and how she can support you. Offer to do the same for her or to consent to what your partner needs for the time you do spend together. You may also want to write a contract for yourself or your boss. The contract could be an actual document that you create for yourself or share with your partner or your boss, or it could simply serve to help you organize your thoughts and frame the conversations you have to advocate your solitude. Actually creating a contract communicates the value you place on solitude and the importance it will have in your conversations. Here is a sample contract for the intimate other:

Dear Richard,

My needs for routine solitude are important. They are not frivolous or optional. I need you to understand, respect, and actively support my solitude needs. When I request solitude, you agree not to take it personally. My request stems from my own need for self-care and does not reflect my feelings for you.

On my side, I pledge to be fully present during the times we share together. Getting enough solitude is integral for my ability to do this. When I have overextended my energy socially, I will need extra time to retreat and recharge my batteries. Especially if I have made these social efforts on behalf of others or work, I will make a distinct effort to schedule quality connection time with you after I have recovered.

Thank you for your understanding.

Signed and Dated:

Vanessa, January 6, 2015

Witnessed and Dated:

Richard, January 6, 2015

Here is a sample contract for yourself:

Dear Self,

I know that you need ample and regular doses of solitude, yet sometimes I forget this or don't give it the priority that it requires. I also know that when I don't honor my solitude needs, I will pay the price later on. Given this knowledge, I pledge to make solitude a priority. I commit myself to the following solitude activities on a regular basis: meditation four times per week, a quiet ride home from work with no phone calls or radio twice per week, and at least one solitary creativity-related activity each week, such as going to a gallery, museum, or café by myself. When circumstances conspire and I cannot honor these commitments, I will endeavor to make them up as soon as I can.

Signed and Dated:

Me, January 6, 2015

Here is a sample contract for your boss:

Dear Boss,

As I have explained to you, it is stressful for me to work in an open-plan office. It is hard to concentrate and difficult to be creative. The lack of privacy cuts into the solitude I need to stay fresh, open, and efficient. To offset these stresses, I request having access to a private office for at least ten hours per week. I also request having the option to work from home one day per week. Flexibility on these two issues will help me to be more productive, healthier, and happier at work.

On my end, I will take extra special care of my solitude needs outside of the office, in particular by practicing mindfulness meditation, so that I can maximize my productivity while at work. When I am in the open space, I will use headphones to create a sense of solitude, and I will also employ a signaling system to communicate to others how open I am to interruptions.

Signed and Dated:

Me, January 6, 2015

Witnessed and Dated:

Boss, January 6, 2015

For more on the "signaling system" mentioned in the letter above, see "Signal Your Availability" in chapter 7.

Solitude Contract

_____

_____

_____

_____

_____

Claiming Solitude: "In Silence"

You may be able to claim absolute solitude in the wilderness, but it may be hard to find a true wilderness experience, even if you are so inclined. So what do you do then? A tradition employed at the Kripalu Center for Yoga and Health in Stockbridge, Massachusetts, may provide you with a helpful approach. At the center, many workshops can occur simultaneously at any given time. Most of them are not conducted in silence. However, if you want to be in silence, you wear a nametag that simply reads, "In loving silence." This helps you to create solitude.

Perhaps you'll need a similar sign if you head out into the wild. The moose, bear, and deer won't read it, but it will give other human beings a heads-up that you are seeking solitude and they should not interpret your lack of socializing as being rude. Imagine walking through the world in this way. For example, you could wear a nametag with the message, "I appreciate your interest in me, but I am practicing solitude."

Create your own version of the "In Silence" nametag:

_____

Quiet Solitude: The Power of the Meditation Retreat

The ancient custom of the meditation retreat is a welcome respite in today's world of noise, clamor, and talk. One type of retreat is the vipassana meditation retreat, a tradition within Theravada Buddhism. Participants on these retreats take a vow of "noble silence": a commitment to not communicate verbally or nonverbally nor to indulge in other sources of information, such as reading, writing, and, of course, using their smartphone. The retreat is a radical departure from the noisiness of everyday life and requires a big commitment of time, energy, and social capital (to set aside your daily life for ten days requires the help of others).

Profoundly different from your day-to-day environment, everything at the retreat supports your silence. The staff, volunteers, and fellow retreatants collaborate to create an environment supportive to meditation practice. Your meals are prepared for you with loving attention; you just have to show up and eat mindfully. At one retreat center—the Insight Meditation Society in Barre, Massachusetts—retreatants, called "yogis," also do a brief work practice. Here you do a household chore, such as washing dishes, sweeping floors, or cleaning bathrooms, again in silence. This work practice is an opportunity to bridge your meditation practice with the demands of everyday life. Even when your job puts you next to other people, you do the work in silence. It is solitude in action.

The retreat provides quiet but not complete solitude; you sit in meditation with many others. You'd have to go meditate in a cave to find complete solitude. Salmon and Matarese (2014) highlight the need for social support when investigating your inner experience. This need for social support arises from the fact that, from an evolutionary perspective, humans have a tendency to have very active minds. The presence of others can provide a comforting context that allows the mind to relax into the present moment. This support is realized even if the members never say a word to each other. You'll feel the presence of other people as you sit in the meditation hall, hour after hour. You'll walk side by side with others during the walking meditation periods. Yet, despite this physical closeness, each retreatant acts as the guardian of solitude for every other retreatant. If you're interested in this type of retreat, see the Resources at the end of the book for more information.

The Mini-Solitude Retreat

On a regular basis, take a day for solitude. Plan this day so you don't have any formal commitments—no phone calls, appointments, or tasks that require going into public places (like grocery shopping). The goal is to have a day where you can be with yourself in an unstructured way. Even having one thing on the schedule can influence the entire day. Charles Dickens bemoaned that "the mere consciousness of an engagement will sometimes worry a whole day" (Hartley 2012, 293). How will you fill the vast expanse of this day? You can venture out into nature, where solitude may be easier to find (unless you run into other nature seekers). You can arrange a quiet day at home when the other members of your household are busy or away. You can even check into a hotel, which gives you the added dimension of being away from the "noise" of familiar surroundings. Meditation is a great way to fill your day of solitude. Think about how you would like to spend this day and take some notes here:

_____

_____

_____

_____

Come back to this section after you have taken this day. What did you learn about yourself? What will you change for the next solitude retreat? When can you commit to the next one? What came up for you in this day without the influence of other people?

_____

_____

_____

_____

Concluding Thoughts

Solitude is hard to come by in this hectic, extrovert-dominated, and digitally connected culture, yet it is a crucial, often overlooked component of introvert self-care. This chapter may have revealed the solitude deficits in your life and how you can address them, or it may have been a reminder of the value, power, and sweet necessity of solitude. You can embrace solitude as a valid way of being. Solitude is indispensable for an introspective life. It is impossible to live an awakened life without pockets of solitude. Mindfulness can be your portable solitude companion, even when you cannot withdraw from the rest of humanity. And when you do get the chance to have some solitary peace and quiet, what better time is there to do some mindfulness practice? As the world gets more and more digitally connected, the need for nurturing solitude will become more and more critical. At the same time, it's easy to get pulled into digital connectivity and forget the more basic need for solitude. Regular unplugging will serve you well, and your regular meditation practice can provide this unconnected respite of peace.

Chapter 6

Managing Your Energy: Self-Care and Restoration

Being an introvert in an extrovert world can be exhausting. The very same interactions that give extroverts energy drain you. To offset these energy expenditures, you need to take extra special care of yourself—with an emphasis on protecting and restoring your energy. We've already discussed the need to nurture yourself with ample doses of quiet and solitude (see chapters 3 and 5). In this chapter, we'll explore introvert self-care more deeply as we look at energy management tools, strategies, and practices that will help you to mindfully balance and sustain your energy as well as maintain your vitality.

If we think of energy like food, extroverts are those people who can eat anything they want and not gain weight. They can engage in all the activities that you find draining and not only enjoy themselves but also be energized by them! (Of course, they may eat a lot of junk food as a result of this ability to eat anything with impunity.) You are like a person on a diet who needs to be calorie conscious, but the calories we're talking about here aren't food calories but "calories" of energy. So, if you eat the equivalent of a piece of chocolate cake by going to a party, you'll have to watch your calories afterward—perhaps by skipping the next social function you're invited to. As an introvert, you must carefully nurture and care for your energy. Because of this, you eat less junk food and nourish yourself on quality sustenance.

So, how exactly do you care for your energy? By *RPM*. You probably know the term "rpm," which refers to the revolutions per minute of an engine. Here, as a way of caring for yourself, I want to introduce you to a different kind of RPM, which means *respect*, *protect*, and *modulate* your energy. You *respect* your energy through monitoring and balancing what builds your energy and what depletes it. You *protect* your energy by making choices that reflect your values and maintain your self-care. You mindfully *modulate* your energy to restore it as you navigate through the stresses and activities of each day. Because caring for your energy is so important, let's take a closer look now at each aspect of RPM.

Respect Your Energy: Monitor and Balance Activities

To respect your energy, you have to both monitor and balance it. By "monitor," I mean that it's important to be aware of how you spend your energy: What exhausts or depletes you? What energizes or restores you? Respect also requires balance—that is, matching the energy that moves out of you with the energy that comes in. A useful notion of balance comes from the Eastern symbol of the Tao. This symbol shows the relationship between two basic forces that are inherent to *everyone*: yin and yang. Yin is introverted energy; yang is extroverted energy. Yin is dark, interior, and collected. Yang is light, exterior, and dispersive. As Carl Jung said, "There is no such thing as a pure extrovert or a pure introvert. Such a man would be in a lunatic asylum" (Evans 1964, 70). While these forces, and by extension introversion and extroversion, are part of everyone, each person has a different balance and expression of these energies.

Notice how there is a bit of yin in the yang and a bit of yang in the yin. As an introvert, you may not be split down the middle with perfect symmetry as the symbol shows. The challenge is to find a balance of introversion and extroversion that works for you. This symbol suggests that you can nurture that bit of extrovert within yourself and try to bring your energies into a relative balance. For example, if you must behave like an extrovert at work, then you will need to spend time recovering your energy by engaging with more introverted activities. Keeping an energy ledger will help you know how to keep your life balanced.

Your Energy Ledger: Keeping an Introvert-Extrovert Activity Balance

To complete your energy ledger (a blank version of which can be found later in this section, and online at http://www.newharbinger.com/36101), first identify each of your activities for each day, determine whether each is an introvert or an extrovert activity, and then enter it into the appropriate column. Next, for each activity, rate its intensity using a scale of 1 to 10 (with 1 as the least intense and 10 being the most intense). The intensity is a combination of the time involved, the energy you spent on the activity, and the benefit you derived from it or the stress it caused. Not every introvert or extrovert activity will have the same value in terms of time and energy spent and benefit gained or stress induced. (In the sample energy ledger later in this section, the intensity number is given in parentheses after the activity.) Finally, determine your "balance quotient"—that is, how balanced your activities are in terms of introvert or extrovert energy. To calculate this, first add together the intensity ratings for your introverted activities, assign the tally a *positive* number, and place the total at the bottom of the Introverted Activities column. Next, add together the intensity ratings for your extroverted activities but assign the tally a *negative* number and place the total at the bottom of the Extroverted Activities column. In the sample ledger, Monday had 10 intensity units for introverted activities (+10) and 16 intensity units for extroverted activities (–16). Now—here's where you have to remember some of your old math skills!—add together the intensity units: 10 + (–16) = –6. The balance quotient for that day is therefore –6, which means you have an extrovert imbalance (that is, more extroverted than introverted activities).

My Energy Ledger: Introvert-Extrovert Activity Balance—A Sample

	Introverted (I) Activities with Intensity Rating	Extroverted (E) Activities with Intensity Rating	Balance Quotient
Monday	30-minute workout at gym (4) Quick 20-minute meditation before going out (6)	Work-related travel (4) Presentation at work (7) Celebration after work (5)	+10 introvert units plus −16 extrovert units = −6 extrovert units (extrovert imbalance)
Tuesday	Meditated on the plane after excusing myself from conversation (5) Returned home from airport without going back to office, read, and took a nap. Had the house to myself. (9)	Work-related travel stuck next to talkative passenger (6)	+14 introvert units plus −6 extrovert units = +8 introvert units (introvert surplus)
Total	Monday (−6) + Tuesday (+8) = +3 units Balance restored with a positive introvert surplus quotient of 3 units		

Your calculations do not have to be rocket-science precise. Don't agonize over rating an activity. Is it a 6 or 7? Make your best guess, and over time you'll have a better sense of what works. Look at your tallies. What is your ratio of introverted to extroverted activities in the course of a typical week? Are you in the "black" (that is, your introverted activities balance or exceed your extroverted activities) or are you in the "red" (your extroverted activities exceed your introverted activities)? How well-balanced are you at the end of the week? If you run a deficit, you will need to introduce more introverted activities to bring your life closer to balance. On the other hand, if you don't have to be extroverted at work, then you may find that you need to bring more extroverted activities into your life. Balance, for you, may not be "zero." You may need an introvert surplus each week to feel whole. If you have been out of balance for a long while, transitioning to a more balanced rhythm of life may be difficult at first. It's important to be aware, however, that you can adapt to almost any situation—even one that is very imbalanced. When imbalance occurs for a long time, it may become hidden; it's just what "normal" feels like. The other tools in this chapter will help you find balance by prioritizing and monitoring your energy.

My Energy Ledger: Introvert-Extrovert Activity Balance

	Introverted (I) Activities with Intensity Rating	Extroverted (E) Activities with Intensity Rating	Balance Quotient
Monday			
Tuesday			
Wednesday			
Thursday			
Friday			
Saturday			
Sunday			
Total			

Once you've monitored your introverted and extroverted activities and completed your energy ledger, you may find that, in addition to balancing introverted and extroverted activities, you may also need to protect your energy by embracing your limits. Let's explore how you can do that.

Protect Your Energy: Embrace Your Limits

Energy is the power to do things. It is motivation, inclination, and movement. Energy is an unseen force. In the Chinese practice of qigong, energy is understood as the invisible forces, such as gravity and electromagnetic radiation, that surround you. Energy can't be measured, but it can have a profound effect on the quality of your life. If you don't protect your energy by setting limits on activities, it won't be available when you need it the most. When your energy is low, activities you find difficult as an introvert will feel even more difficult. If you expend too much energy extroverting, you may find that you don't enjoy the activities that you usually enjoy. Without good energy, life can become a pale shadow of its potential vividness.

You may be caught in a trap where life looks like a never-ending to-do list without enough time to do everything. Pushing yourself too hard for too long results in fatigue, exhaustion, and burnout. Tony Schwartz (2013), founder and CEO of the Energy Project and best-selling author, wrote in the *New York Times,* "Paradoxically, the best way to get more done may be to spend more time doing less. A new and growing body of multidisciplinary research shows that strategic renewal—including daytime workouts, short afternoon naps, longer sleep hours, more time away from the office, and longer, more frequent vacations—boosts productivity, job performance and, of course, health." Use the tools in this chapter to find opportunities for *energy renewal* in your day.

According to psychologist Marti Olsen Laney (2002), introverts are like rechargeable batteries while extroverts are like solar panels. For extroverts, socializing is like the sun; it charges them up. But you cannot recharge a rechargeable battery by placing it in the sun. It must be taken out of service and plugged into a power source. So, if introverts are rechargeable batteries, what is that power source that you need to plug into? It's mindfulness. Mindfulness gives you the ability to recharge your batteries anywhere and anytime without complete withdrawal or shutdown. Mindfulness practice is, in essence, the study of energy. By bringing curious attention to the unfolding of your experience moment by moment, you are studying the flow of energy and also tapping into it at the same time. This connection to your energy allows you to move in ways that will benefit you—you'll feel rested, recharged, and renewed.

Mindfulness can also help you to identify where your best energy is during the course of the day. Spend the next few days monitoring your energy level as you move through the day. Keep track on the chart provided. This information will help you to better protect your energy. You'll likely notice variations throughout the day. Identify your prime energy times, and see if any patterns emerge. You may notice, for example, lulls in your energy that come in the midafternoon hours. Monitoring your energy will help you to create a strategy for managing your day. When you have the ability to arrange certain activities, it makes sense to do the tasks that *require* the most energy at the times when you *have* the most energy. If you try to do difficult extrovert activities during a period of low energy, you may not perform your best.

A sample energy chart is also provided here. Notice how energy dips in the middle of the afternoon. If your chart looks like this, you will want to plan for these variations in energy. If you know your energy will be predictably low at a particular time, plan for this by not scheduling activities that requires your best attention at that time. For instance, if having meetings require your best energy, consider scheduling them at times other than your energy low-point in the mid- to late afternoon. During that interval, do something that does not require much thinking energy. Organize your desk, clean your office, or do other low-energy-level tasks that won't tax you very much.

Energy Chart

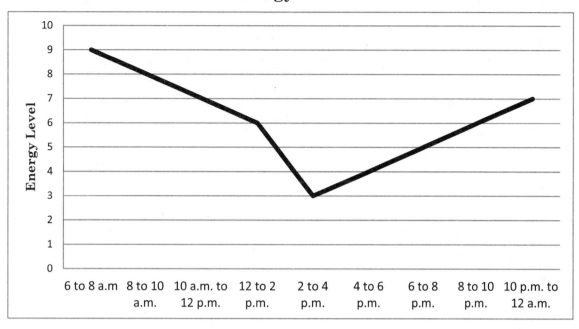

Now take a few minutes to do your own energy chart for a typical work day. Repeat this process over several days. When do you experience your best energy? When is your energy lowest? Is it consistent from day to day?

Energy Chart

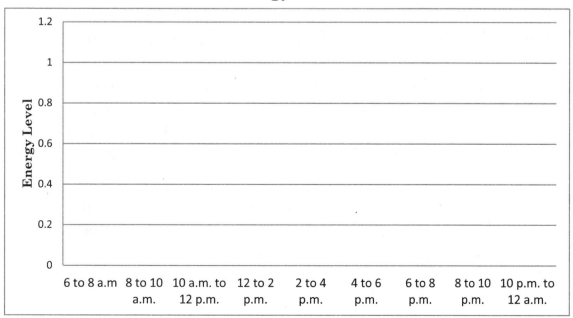

Now complete another chart for a nonworkday.

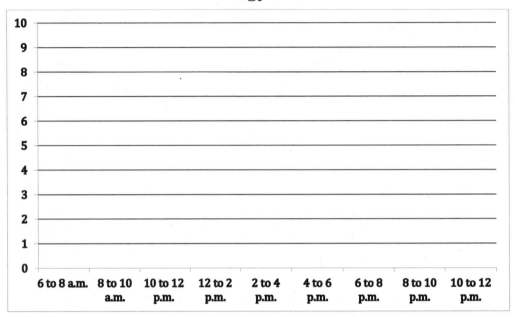

Energy Chart

Do you notice any differences between the workday and the nonworkday?

Energy is not fixed. Some activities build it and others drain it. The substances that you put into your body and the activities in which you engage every day will either build or drain your energy. In the table that follows is a list of common substances and activities. As you engage with these, notice how they affect your energy. They may inspire good-quality energy or poor-quality energy. For instance, caffeine may give you energy, but it does so at the cost of nervousness, edginess, and possible sleep disruption. If there are substances and activities that are important in your life but that are not listed here, please add them.

Substances That May Affect Energy

Substance	Builds Energy	Drains Energy	Neutral	Quality
Alcohol				
Artificial sweeteners				
Caffeine				
Chocolate				
Food additives (e.g., MSG)				
Junk food				
Marijuana				
Sugar				
Tobacco				

Activities That May Affect Energy

Activity	Builds Energy	Drains Energy	Neutral	Quality
Eating certain foods				
Exercising				
Forgetting to eat				
Going to movies				
Meditating				
Overeating				
Reading				
Sex				
Sleeping				
Watching television/video				

What did you learn from this exercise? Are you surprised by the things that drain your energy? Can you commit to doing less of these in the future? Likewise, if you've discovered things that build your energy, can you bring these more into your life?

_____

_____

_____

_____

_____

Introverts face particular challenges in protecting their energy in socially demanding situations, especially those that also bring a high degree of stimulation. The next exercise looks at these situations. See if you can estimate how many units of energy you expend on each activity. The scale of energy units is 0 to 100. If you used all 100 units, you'd be in a coma on life support. As with the Energy Ledger, this is not meant to be a precise scientific measurement, so just estimate as best as you can. For example, if that presentation at work wipes you out, you may have spent between 30 and 50 units. Now, how long does it take you to get back to your *energy baseline*—that is, your typical level of energy where you are neither drained nor have an abundance of energy? The answer to this question, in large part, depends on how you spend that time between the event and your return to normal. Are you engaging with energy-restoring activities (we'll explore these in the next section), or are you draining your energy further? Understanding the "cost" of the activities you engage in on a regular basis can be key for developing strategies to better protect and manage your energy.

Energy Expenditures

Situation	Energy Units Expended	Recovery Time
Attending a large party		
Being in a chaotic, loud environment		
Doing nonstop activities with kids		
Experiencing conflict with significant other		
Having family visit		
Making a presentation at work		
Meeting new people		
Participating in watercooler conversations		
Taking part in holiday activities		
Traveling		
Other		

Becoming familiar with the substances and activities that impact your energy can help you to plan how to spend your energy as you do the things you need to do in the course of your days, weeks, and your entire life. This is especially true for the challenges you face at work, where large demands may be placed on your energy. You can become an expert in restoring your energy when it is drained by the things you must do. The next section will help you to develop this expertise.

Modulate Your Energy: Introvert Restoration Techniques

As an introvert living in an extrovert world, your energy is likely to be overtaxed much of the time. To maximize your energy, you'll need a repertoire of introvert restoration techniques that will help you to *modulate* your energy—that is, making fine- and large-stroke adjustments to your behavior to keep your energy in a good range. You need to be true to your authentic desires and spend time engaged in actions consistent with them. The more of these activities that you have in your life, the better equipped you'll be at any moment and in any given situation to find something to support or enhance your energy needs. Practicing these restoration techniques on a regular basis will help you to support your energy and keep it from being depleted.

The table that follows gives a list of activities that introverts may find restorative. Put a check mark next to the ones that you do on a regular basis. Fill in other activities that you find restorative that are not on this list.

Restorative Activities

Activity	Frequency
☐ Arrange a day of silence	
☐ Attend a lecture and sit in the back	
☐ Curl up with a good book	
☐ Curl up with your iPad and watch a movie	
☐ Do tai chi	
☐ Go for a run, hike, or bike ride	
☐ Go for a walk in the country	
☐ Go to a coffee shop with a friend to hang out	
☐ Go to a movie	
☐ Go to a play	
☐ Meditate	
☐ Practice qigong	
☐ Practice yoga	
☐ Ride a motorcycle	
☐ Sit in a coffee shop and read/write	
☐ Take a drive (in the country, near the water, on the shore)	
☐ Visit an art gallery, museum, or craft shop	
☐	
☐	

Your repertoire of restoration techniques can be like a living document: always being revised, updated, and expanded. The more you practice these things, the more available they will be at the times when you most need them—when your energy is flagging.

Formal Practice: *The Recovery Meditation*

This guided imagery meditation practice can be a helpful addition to mindfulness practices when your energy has been exhausted. It can help you to establish a portable sanctuary to protect and nurture you whenever the extroverted world has gotten to be too much.

Get into your meditation posture. Bring your attention to your breathing and your body. Let your mind settle into this moment. Imagine being enveloped in vapor—its cloaking anonymity comforts you. You are hidden as you move through the world. By surrounding yourself in this protective vapor, the outside world cannot affect you as much. You can give this vapor a color, or imagine it shrouding you in the soothing aroma of lavender or some other scent. You are safe and invisible in this spacious vapor. It forms a protective bubble around you.

Some occasions require something more robust. You need the protection of wood. If this is true for you now, imagine that you are encased in soft, smooth wood. Wood is impenetrable and also soundproof. The potential disadvantage of wood is linked to its advantage: its protectiveness comes at the cost of mobility. You are hunkered down in deep recovery mode. Enjoy this immobility and feel your energy restoring slowly. With each inhalation, energy comes in, and with each exhalation, you let go of fatigue. Keep breathing in this way until you feel your energy rising.

In severe circumstances, you may need to put a protective layer of armor over the wood. Not much else can get done. If this is true for you now, imagine that you are wrapped in an impenetrable armor. Enjoy being inaccessible to people, tasks, and anything other than restoring your energy. Give this your top priority and just breathe in silence and stillness.

When you feel restored, open your eyes, and resume your normal activities.

Meditation Reflection

Take a few moments to reflect on this practice. Where do you need to restore your energy? In what situations might you do this practice? Can you think of other images that will aid you in your effort to restore your energy?

_____

_____

_____

_____

Dealing with People: Your Social Energy

The poet David Whyte cautioned in his poem "The Sweet Darkness" that we may want to reconsider any relationship or any situation in our life that does not increase our sense of aliveness. This is an important message for introverts. How do the people in your life affect your energy?

In the People and Energy Chart provided, list the people in your life. Next, consider how each person affects your energy: Does she build or drain your energy? Does he make you want to crawl into a cave, or does he help you feel more connected to the world? For each relationship, in the Discretion column, note whether your contact with this person is elective or necessary. In other words, can you exercise discretion over the time you spend together? If the person is your boss, you may not have much discretion, but if the person is a so-called friend who turns out to be an energy vampire, you probably do have a choice. In the final column, think about strategies you might engage to help with these contacts. If the person builds your energy, plan to spend more time with her. If the person drains energy, can you set some limits on your contact with him? Another set of strategies involves preparing for and debriefing from stressful contacts. Your restoration techniques can help you to prepare for a draining encounter and help you to recover afterward. For instance, one of your restoration techniques will be mindfulness practice. After a draining encounter, you can do a few minutes of mindfulness practice, feeling the sensations from that encounter in your body and breathing with them. You can also be proactive and do a few minutes of mindfulness before you go into that situation, which may actually help to lessen its draining impact.

People and Energy Chart

Person's Name	Builds or Drains Energy?	Discretion	Strategies

Sleeping Well: The Restorative Power of Good Sleep Hygiene

If you are like most Americans, you are not getting enough sleep. Sleep deprivation is like putting your introversion on steroids. Sensitivities are magnified, social obligations become more draining, and your thinking slows down.

Sleep is critical. Scientists don't completely understand all the functions of sleep, but they do know that it is involved in energy restoration, memory consolidation, and other regulatory functions. Humans need an average of eight hours of sleep, but your sleep needs may vary. Some people are long sleepers and require more than eight hours; some people are short sleepers and require less. How many hours do you need? When you think about this question, consider what you *actually* need rather than what you would like to need. You may rationalize that if you sleep less, you can get more of your to-do list done. But be honest with yourself. Starting tonight, and using the Sleep Habits form shown, monitor your sleep for the next week. (Copies of the form can be downloaded at http://www.newharbinger.com/36101 as you need them.) Fill out the form the next day. You can fill out the first few columns in the morning and the last two later in the day.

Note your bedtime and how long it takes you to fall asleep. (If it takes you more than twenty minutes, see the next section on dealing with insomnia.) Indicate what time you woke up and how long you slept. Rate how restful your sleep was by indicating your energy level the next day using a scale of 1 to 10, where 1 is extremely low energy (you are barely able to keep your eyes open and head up) and 10 is the best energy you've ever had (your energy is boundless and you're ready to take on any challenge). Also, note if you experienced an energy crash in the afternoon. Mammals, including humans, have an approximate twenty-four-hour clock called the *circadian rhythm*, and it goes through roughly two twelve-hour cycles. Among other things, body temperature and energy fluctuate throughout the day. Most people experience the circadian low from about 2:00 to 5:00 p.m. every day. If you are short of sleep, you may feel low energy at that time of day and want to take a nap.

Sleep Habits

Day	Bedtime	Length of Time It Took to Fall Asleep	Waking Time	Sleep Duration	Energy Level (1–10)	Afternoon Crash? Y/N

If you find that you are consistently tired, you are probably not getting enough sleep. Try to lengthen your window of time that you actually sleep and monitor your sleep for another week. You should feel more rested and less likely to crash in the afternoon during the circadian rhythm low. If sleep problems persist despite adding more sleep time, you may have a sleep issue and should consult your primary care physician, who may refer you to a sleep specialist.

Sleep Hygiene Checklist

If you are experiencing insomnia (difficulty falling or staying asleep), you can use a variety of techniques to maintain good sleep hygiene. In fact, sleep hygiene is a good idea for everyone because it helps to build your best quality of sleep. Below is a list of what sleep experts recommend. Put a check mark next to the ones you observe.

- ☐ My bedroom is cool and dark.

- ☐ I go to bed and arise at consistent times.

- ☐ I avoid eating heavy meals before going to sleep.

- ☐ I don't consume alcohol, or consume only a moderate amount, and not close to bedtime.

- ☐ I avoid bright lights before bedtime.

- ☐ I avoid vigorous exercise in the evening.

- ☐ I don't allow myself to toss and turn (for more than twenty minutes).

- ☐ I keep technology out of the bedroom (for example, televisions, computers, tablets, and smartphones).

- ☐ I don't nap in the afternoon.

- ☐ I avoid excessive stimulation late at night (for instance, violence on television).

If you have checked all the items on the list, you are practicing great sleep hygiene. Which of the items, if any, do you need to work on?

_____

_____

_____

_____

Dealing with Insomnia

Here are some guidelines for dealing with sleep difficulties:

1. Practice the principles of sleep hygiene in the Sleep Hygiene Checklist.

2. Turn your alarm clock so you can't see it. This limits ambient light, and it also helps to avoid moments of distress when you look at the clock and see that it is 3:42 a.m. and you are not asleep. If you don't know the exact time, you won't be tempted to obsess about how your day is going to be ruined because you were still awake at such and such a time.

3. Observe the "twenty-minute rule." If you have not fallen asleep after twenty minutes, get out of bed and do some nonstimulating activity. (Since you can't see your alarm clock, you'll have to estimate when twenty minutes has elapsed.) Drink a small glass of warm milk; do walking meditation in a dimly lit part of the house; do some gentle stretching, yoga, or qigong; or take a hot shower or bath. When you feel sleepy, make another attempt to fall asleep. Repeat as needed. The purpose of this exercise is to avoid associating your bed with the frustration of not getting to sleep.

4. Meditate. The one exception to the twenty-minute rule is to stay in bed and practice meditation. If you are lying on your back, this is a good posture to do a body scan (see "Formal Practice: Body Scan" in this chapter). You can think

131

of this practice as "beditation." Chances are, you will fall asleep in the midst of your body scan. If you don't fall asleep, at least you have gotten the restful benefits of the meditation practice. While there are no scientific studies to confirm it, anecdotal evidence suggests that minutes of meditation can be exchanged with minutes of sleep. The worst-case scenario is that you meditate all night and receive all the benefits that come with practice.

Awareness of the Body: Physical Restoration

The body can be a powerful resource for restoration. These resources will be explored below, starting with a meditation technique known as the body scan.

The body scan is a staple of mindfulness meditation. It is a straightforward technique that concentrates attention on the physical aspects of the body in a systematic, nonjudgmental, and curious way. The body scan helps to restore energy by connecting attention with the energy of the body. The Buddha practiced a version of it in his process of awakening. Jon Kabat-Zinn (1990) introduced it as a secular practice in 1979 at the Stress Reduction Clinic at the University of Massachusetts Medical School, thereby initiating the incorporation of mindfulness into medical settings, something that is ubiquitous today.

There are many different ways to practice the body scan. You can strike different postures: sitting or lying down are two common ones. You can move through the body systematically, examining each part of the body as if you were doing a guided tour. Or you can move your attention to whatever is most prominent in the body. You can also do both, starting with the more structured approach and then opening to whatever arises. Both of these approaches have benefit. By systematically exploring the body, you develop an intimacy with your body; you notice how things are changing moment by moment. This can help you to manage discomfort, pain, and strong emotions. The ability to attend to whatever presents itself physically helps you develop insight and wisdom.

Formal Practice: *Body Scan*

Get into a comfortable posture. This could be sitting upright with your legs crossed, or it could be, as is often done with a body scan, in a lying-down position. Now set your intention to practice, setting aside your usual thoughts and concerns to focus on what is happening now. Start by noticing your breathing. Feel the physical sensations of your breath. First, at the tip of your nose, feel the contact between the air and the nose. Notice movement and temperature. Try to regard these sensations with an objective interest, neither for nor against them. Keep your attention keen without getting rigid, tense, or tight. Notice how these sensations change moment by moment. Whenever your attention moves away from the sensations in the nose, gently usher your awareness back to the nose and begin again. Explore all the sensations you can notice as you scan through the rest of the nose. Then seek sensations on the surface and from within the tissues of the nose, the mouth, the throat, and down into your lungs, chest, and abdomen. Spend time with each region. Don't rush. Feel the sense of breath as a whole—from the tip of your nose down to the bottom of your lungs. Notice all the sensations you can notice. Your attention is now grounded on the breath and you can return to this sense of the breath whenever your attention wanders away or whenever something gets too intense somewhere else in the body.

Now, move your attention to the toes of your left foot. Explore the toes as you explored your breathing—with interest and precision. Notice any sensations on the surface or within the toes. You will notice some places that have a lot of sensations and others that don't seem to have many sensations at all. This is fine. Just notice what you can notice and keep bringing your attention back whenever it moves away. Explore the toes, focusing on resistance (any sense of pressure or contact with other toes, clothing, the floor), movement, and temperature. From the toes, move your attention into the wider foot, the top of the foot, the sole of the foot, and into the ankle and lower leg. Explore the calf and the shin as you move toward the knee. Spend some time with the knee before you move through the upper leg, feeling the thigh. Once you have examined all the parts of the leg, feel it as a whole, from the tips of your toes to the top of the leg. Now move your attention to the toes of the right foot as you let the left leg move into the background of awareness. Repeat the process with the right toes, foot, and leg. Feel the entire leg after you have visited all of its parts.

Now bring your attention back to both legs and feel your lower body. Notice any sensations with an open curiosity. If your mind generates thoughts about what it is finding or not finding, redirect it to some sensation you can appreciate now. Move from the legs to the pelvic region, exploring your hips, buttocks, and genitals. Remember, if at any time some sensation feels like it is more than you can handle in the moment, you can shift your attention back to breathing. Explore this region with the same open curiosity with which you examined your breathing and legs. Move from the pelvic region into the lower back, middle back, and upper back. Feel the back as a whole. Now move into your abdomen, the lower abdomen, where you may feel your breath moving, and explore your abdomen on the surface, as well as any sensations coming from within. As you move through the torso, you'll find breathing happening in many places there. Once you have touched on all the parts of the torso, feel it as a whole, bringing in awareness of the back and breathing. Spend some time with the torso.

Now you can move into your arms. If you have time, you can explore each shoulder, arm, and hand individually, or you can scan them together. Start with your shoulders and move awareness down toward your fingers. Once you have reached the fingers, bring awareness back over the entire arm (or arms). From the arms, move into the neck and throat, and once more find the breath moving there. Now spend some time investigating the head and face. Examine each part of your face: mouth, tongue, teeth, gums, chin, cheeks, nose, eyes, forehead, and scalp. Feel the entire head.

You have now been through the entire body. Feel the body as a whole for a few cycles of your breath. Once you have grounded yourself in the entire body, spend some time sweeping attention through the body, from the top of the head to the tips of your fingers and toes and back up again. Experiment with different speeds of sweeping from very slow to rather fast. Spend five or ten minutes sweeping through the body.

Once you have done some sweeping, open your attention to the body as a whole, and sit and watch. Move your attention to whatever sensations arise. Stay with them until another prominent sensation emerges somewhere else in the body. Keep your attention fluid with no particular agenda.

You can also feel your body breathing. This awareness includes all the sensations associated directly with breathing and also a greater sense of the entire body. Notice how the boundary lines between the parts of the body involved with breathing can be blurry. Where do the lungs end and the rest of the torso begin? When you have concentrated your mind, you can feel the breath filling the entire torso, neck, and head. You can even feel your breath in your arms and legs as the blood carries oxygen throughout the body. You can be a breathing body.

When you are ready, make your transition back to your normal way of being in the world, taking some of your body awareness with you. Feel these bodily sensations as you get up from your practice spot and move through the rest of your day. Remember that you can always return to the body. These sensations are always present and always willing to receive your attention.

Meditation Reflection

Take a few moments to contemplate this practice. What did you discover about your body? Did you feel things that you haven't felt before? Can you feel the residue of bodily sensations as you do this writing exercise?

_____

_____

_____

_____

Now that you are grounded in your body and have started to cultivate this intimacy with its energies, you can turn your attention to your voice. What follows is a way to change your energy by bringing awareness to how you use your voice.

Building Your Energy Through the Hidden Power of Your Voice

The voice is an underappreciated instrument for energy and emotional expression. The voice requires good energy and also produces good energy when engaged properly. Many people misuse their voice and suffer from chronic voice strain. Our culture values a deep, "macho," assertive voice, but this is often an inefficient way to speak that puts stress on the vocal cords. Introverts are often soft-spoken. This style of speaking can actually cause physical problems with the voice as well as make the introvert look shy, retiring, or meek. Finding your resonant voice can be beneficial for increasing your presence in social interactions and taking care of your vocal instrument.

A study by Dietrich and Abbot (2012) lends support to the notion that introverts are at higher risk for straining their voices. They compared introverts and extroverts without voice disorders during a public speaking task by measuring the activity in the muscles surrounding the larynx. They found that, during a public speaking task, introverts have more stress in their voice than extroverts, which was not explained by anxiety. This type of muscle activation puts individuals at risk for voice disorders, such as muscle tension dysphonia. The introverts in the study also showed poorer voice-related quality of life as measured by the Vocal Handicap Index (VHI). The VHI measures the functional voice characteristics of quietness of the voice, voice projection, the physical aspect of running out of air, and the emotional aspects of being embarrassed to repeat what was said and feeling tense while talking because of self-consciousness concerning the voice. The findings of this study confirm the subjective impressions of introverts, including this author (see the section "My Story"). The quietness of the voice and the lack of projection forces more vocal effort, which leads to muscle strain. This strain may not result in a voice disorder unless you, the introvert, are also exposed to risk factors such as needing to use your voice at work, overusing your voice consistently in personal life, or a general lack of physical well-being.

Proper speaking requires good breath support. Make sure that you breathe with your diaphragm. The diaphragm is a wall of muscle at the bottom of the lungs. When you fill your lower lungs with air, the diaphragm will be engaged; as it contracts, it will appear as if you are breathing into your belly, which expands. There is a simple test to see how you are breathing. You can do this sitting or lying down. Place your right hand on your chest and your left hand on your belly. Which hand is moving as you breathe? When the diaphragm is engaged, your left hand only will move. See if you can do this now.

Diaphragmatic breathing requires practice before it becomes your natural way of breathing, but it is a relaxing way of breathing. Slow, full breathing is associated with the relaxing or parasympathetic branch of the autonomic nervous system, while rapid, shallow breathing is associated with the energizing or sympathetic branch (think of the fight-or-flight response). If you breathe diaphragmatically, your voice will be better supported.

There are other simple exercises that can support your voice. The "uhm-hum" exercise is one of them. Place your fingers on your sternum and make a humming sound with your mouth closed. Move your fingers up and down as you hum. This will give you a sense of your resonant tone. Now take a full breath and say "uhm-hum," followed by the numbers "one, two, three, four, five." Repeat "uhm-hum" and another five numbers each round all the way to fifty. A great way to support speaking is to learn how to sing.

Speaking is just like exercising. If you have a presentation to make, you can do vocal warm-up exercises before you speak and cool-down exercises afterward. You can get these exercises from the Internet, or from your singing instructor, voice coach, or speech therapist.

Your voice requires energy and also creates energy. When your voice is in the right place and has energy behind it, your facial expression is brighter, too, and this creates a potent energizing combination in social situations. Extroverts may do this more naturally, but you can practice elevating your energy by developing your voice.

My Story: Finding My Voice

Some years ago, I was experiencing a lot of hoarseness, so I went to see a speech pathologist. She diagnosed me with a functional voice disorder (muscle tension dysphonia). I was using my voice in an inefficient way such that my vocal cords were not closing together. This put strain on the surrounding muscles and, to cope with that strain, I would speak more softly. That, in turn, would make the vocal folds even more inefficient. I had to learn to talk again, to change the energy in my voice, and to move my voice from the lower throat to the space around my nose and mouth. There were many situations where my introverted tendencies would compound my voice dysfunction. I would be soft-spoken when meeting people, and the more strained my voice felt, the more soft-spoken I became. It was hard to break out of the vicious cycle, especially because, as a psychotherapist, I talk for a living. What I discovered was that one of the key factors for leveraging the proper energy placement for my voice is my general energy level. When my energy is low, it is harder to speak in the way my speech therapist taught me to speak.

My voice has become direct feedback about the state of my energy. When my tone gets soft and hushed, I know I am low on energy. I also know I am not using my voice properly if it cracks; it sounds like I am a teenager. Whenever this happens when I am speaking to a group, I joke that I am experiencing delayed-onset puberty. (This always gets a good laugh.) That crack is a signal that I am not providing good breath support for my speaking and that I need to take a full diaphragmatic breath and slow down.

I have also taken singing lessons from renowned singing teacher Bill Reed. I have learned how to leverage my voice for singing and speaking as well as how to care for my voice with warm-ups and cool-downs. Singing gives expression to the voice and helps me to find the right energy for singing and speaking.

The voice is a powerful instrument and can be used to build or diminish energy. As an introvert, you'll need to pay special attention to your voice, and with that awareness, you can make your voice work for you as a vehicle not only for communication but also for working with your energy from moment to moment. Despite your best efforts, you will still experience times when your energy is drained or depleted because you haven't had an opportunity to replenish energy. The next section will explore what to do when you get stuck in an energy emergency.

Coping with an Energy Emergency

You may be stuck in a meeting or in a social obligation and find yourself flagging. Use your mindfulness skills in this situation to transform your low energy from an emergency into something that is just an experience. When you are exhausted, this registers as information in the body. Your brain recognizes this particular pattern of sensations as fatigue, exhaustion, or depletion. This pattern is associated with a negative feeling—the body cries out for rest and none is currently available. This awareness gives rise to a story about your current circumstances. You are distressed:

I can't believe I am stuck in this situation—how am I going to cope? The way to cope is to extricate yourself from the painful story and bring your attention into the body. You can do an on-the-spot body scan to explore the pattern of sensations that are in your body. These sensations are the raw material of fatigue—without the story and its anxious implications. Focus on the energy of these sensations, allowing it to be a neutral, even interesting experience. Whenever your find your attention drawn back into the story about how awful this situation is, gently redirect your attention to your body. Investigate these sensations with precision. As with most things, the more familiar you are with the experience, the less scary it will be. By moving from the story to the body, you can transform this difficult situation into an interesting experience. The more you practice mindfulness techniques such as the body scan, the more readily you will be able to move from the story to the body.

Concluding Thoughts

The author and poet David Whyte (2009) says, "Exile and forgetting are natural states for most human beings, but so are remembering and recalling. All tasks are completed through cycles of visitation and absence" (137). Respecting, protecting, and modulating your energy as explored in this chapter will help with the visitations and absences that come and go. Responsibility without rest is a recipe for exhaustion. If you don't unplug from your workday, it is hard to experience rest. This can be difficult if you readily bring your work home. Another big challenge in managing your energy is managing the ebb and flow of energy in your relationships. You can take a cue from elite athletes. They train intensively for a performance and must be careful not to overtrain. Intense training and performance is followed by a period of quiescence. This is how energy is nurtured. Downtime is important to maintain energy. You can get that from the quiet spaces in your life, especially mindfulness meditation. We've explored several ways of nurturing and restoring energy in this chapter. Hopefully, you have found some techniques that work for you. Remember that respecting your energy needs is the foundation of maintaining your energy.

Chapter 7

Special Operating Instructions: The Introvert Mind

Your introvert mind has special gifts, such as concentration and appreciation for solitude, that require special "operating instructions." When you take care of your unique mind, you'll enjoy your mind's assets while minimizing its liabilities. This chapter will explore the introvert's mind, beginning with the perspective of brain science and tying this to methods of mindfulness practice that will help you in your daily life. In particular, you'll learn how to do the "mind scan" and the QUIET method, which will enable you to transform thoughts and feelings on the spot. You will also learn how to handle interruptions and overstimulation. So, let's get started by looking at some recent research on the introvert brain.

The Introvert Brain

Scientists have been looking into the brains of introverts and extroverts with neuroimaging and are beginning to map out some potential differences. The differences in the introvert brain may explain why you feel out of sorts with loud noises, superficial social contacts, and chaotic settings. There is evidence that your introvert brain is already more active than the brains of extroverts around you. Extroverts have a lower level of activation and therefore need higher levels of stimulation to feel engaged. This explains why extroverts like excitement, parties, thrill seeking, and intense activity. You already have a lot of activity in your brain, so you tend to prefer less stimulating environments. All people seek the optimal level of stimulation for themselves, and extroverts and introverts seek to balance that level of stimulation in different ways. To refine this understanding further, there are two major systems in the brain: one that activates behavior and one that inhibits it. Not surprisingly, extroverts are more connected to the activating system than introverts. In other words, extroverts want to "go" and introverts want to "stay"—or "go" with less intensity.

Forsman et al. (2012) found a number of differences in brain structures when comparing introverts and extroverts. While it is tempting to interpret these findings as reflecting true differences in the brains of introverts and extroverts, the authors of this study caution against making this type of conclusion. This and other studies to date have found inconsistent results; different brain structures have been identified in different studies. Future research will no doubt make these findings clearer. With that caveat in mind, Forsman and colleagues' study suggested that the brains of introverts had more gray matter (that is, density of neurons) and white matter (connective tissue), which is consistent with the idea that introvert brains are more active. Given this higher level of activity, introverts don't need as much stimulation as extroverts. These structural findings are consistent with Johnson and colleagues' (1999) study of blood flow that found more activity in the frontal areas of the brain for introverts, which was mentioned in chapter 1. Forsman and colleagues (2012) also found that introverts had more brain volume in a structure that is known to be involved with self-referential thinking. This finding is consistent with the tendency for the introvert to be engaged in the DMN (default mode network), that part of the brain that is responsible for self-referential internal dialogues or stories that we tend to be constantly engrossed with. The extrovert is more engaged in external activity and is not as focused inwardly.

Xu and colleagues (2005) used an MRI procedure to detect levels of neurotransmitters in the brain. They focused on the anterior cingulate, a structure important to attention, controlling behavior, and modulating emotions. They found differences between introverts and extroverts in the level of glutamate and other neurotransmitters, again suggesting increased levels of activation in introverts.

Given your brain's tendency to be more active, it makes sense to become familiar with this activity so that you can befriend it. The following exercise will help you to do that.

Informal Practice: *Getting Intimate with Being Stimulated*

Since your brain is bound to be more active than the extrovert brain, studying how your body responds to excessive stimulation can help you to become more comfortable with the way you are built. Examining these sensations with mindful attention helps you respond in a more accepting way to excessive stimulation. When you understand your physical responses, you can be more accepting of what happens to you and more skillful in how you adapt to these changes in energy. Do this practice in a noisy, public place (such as an airport terminal) where there is traffic, commotion, or loud noises.

Sit comfortably with your eyes open (or closed, if you prefer) and pay attention to the scene around you. Notice the things in your environment that capture your attention. Notice if you have a sense of heightened physiological activity. Sensations may include increased heart rate, a palpable startle, hair standing on end, a noticeable pulse, a sense of heightened attention, or a mild feeling of anxiety, as if you've had too much coffee. Locate these sensations in your body and observe them objectively. In addition to their location, every sensation has three qualities: intensity, movement, and temperature. Intensity *relates to the sense of pressure, contact, or physical resistance.* Movement *can be an oscillation, vibration, or other subtle feeling.* Temperature *reflects blood flow, so sensations can feel cool or warm. Understand that you are more prone to react physiologically to stimulation. These heightened sensations do not reflect a problem. Your system is more active and will get triggered by the environment more readily. Bring curiosity to every sensation you notice and extricate your attention from any stories you may tell yourself about why you are reacting this way. Your curiosity and the absence of storytelling will help to create a space of non-reactivity, if you will, that can hold all of these sensations. You can put these sensations inside of this space and they can sit there without your needing to do anything about them.*

Getting familiar with your bodily sensations—how you physically react to your environment—will help you to put those sensations in context. This will minimize any tendency to overreact when you experience these sensations. This is mindfulness in action.

There isn't much that you can do to prevent a reaction because this is built into you by your physiology. But your initial reaction is just that—your first reaction. And you can alter what happens after your initial reaction by practicing mindfulness. You do this by observing and accepting the sensations you experience in your body. By accepting the sensations, you don't resist them, and because you don't resist, you do not become tense. Inside, you become more peaceful.

Meditation Reflection

Take a few moments to think about this practice. Do you feel friendlier toward your physiological sensations of reactivity? How is your interpretation of these sensations different now?

_____

_____

_____

_____

You can deepen what you have learned from this informal practice with a formal meditation called the "mind scan." The mind scan will expand your attention beyond the physiological sensations of the body.

Formal Practice: *Mind Scan*

The mind is more than just physiological reactivity stemming from increased brain activity. It is also your senses, imagination, emotion, and thought. A thoroughgoing familiarity with the mind will help you navigate it with more skillfulness. Cultivating intimacy with the mind will help you to be less surprised by your initial reactions in excessively stimulating environments and will help you to respond more mindfully. You can meditate directly on the different aspects of your mind, which will allow the powerful stories you tell yourself to be transformed into "objects" that can be observed with awareness. This transformation diminishes the disruptive impact of these stories. This practice is called the *mind scan*.

The mind can be divided into different components—the subjective and the objective. The chief "products" of the subjective mind are verbal thoughts, mental images, and bodily sensations with an emotional flavoring. The chief products of the objective mind are seeing, hearing, and noticing bodily sensations. All of these will be explored in this practice. You can vary the length of the mind scan by spending more or less time with each part of the mind.

Get into your practice posture, whether this is sitting, standing, or lying down. Set your intentional seat by reorienting yourself from the "business as usual" of the mind—that is, storytelling, reaching into the future and dragging along the past—to a more formal approach to this moment. Refresh your willingness to set aside the stories of the DMN to be with whatever arises. Start with your breathing. Do a quick scan of the body as you did in the body scan meditation, grounding yourself in your body and the present moment. Start by noticing what you can see. If your eyes are closed, you will notice changing patterns of lightness and darkness and perhaps other visual sensations as the light passes through your eyelids. If your eyes are open, then you will see a variety of colors and forms. Try to keep your gaze soft as if you are looking through the objects you see rather than at them. When your mind starts to make associations to what you see, come back to the colors and forms. When your mind starts to tell stories about what you see, again come back to the colors and forms. Try to see without any agenda. After five or ten minutes of this, set aside seeing and move your attention to hearing.

Open your attention to the sounds that are present in your environment. Some of these sounds will be relatively constant, such as the sound of a fan or the heating or cooling system. Other sounds will be episodic, arising and dissolving. Try to bring a curiosity to whatever sounds are appearing and, as with seeing, set aside associations, stories, and agendas and attend to what you hear as it is (sound waves vibrating in your ears and sending signals to your brain).

After five or ten minutes, move your attention back to your body. Do a body sweep from the top of your head to the tips of your fingers and toes, and back from your toe tips and fingertips to the top of your head. Now rest your attention somewhere in the body, perhaps on your breathing, and wait for the arising of any prominent sensations. Direct your attention to these sensations as they arise. Attend to every itch, ache, and discomfort with that same curiosity, interest, and perhaps even fascination. Do this for five or ten minutes.

Now bring your attention to your mind. You will probably sense the mind located somewhere in your head; wherever you sense that it is located is fine. Sit and watch for the arising of thoughts. Thoughts are products of the mind; they arise and vie for attention. You can attend to the thoughts as stories or you can see them as a phenomena happening in the moment. See if you can watch your thoughts in real time. You may find that giving yourself permission to watch your thoughts will make your thoughts shy. They might remain quiet. Or you may find that your attention gets pulled into the story each time you notice a thought. What you'll do next is the most difficult part of this practice. Even when you are pulled into a story, redirect your attention to seeing the thought as a process of the mind, without any concern for its particular content. This is the aim of this practice: shifting attention from contents to the very process of the mind itself. Attend to your thinking process for five or ten minutes.

Now turn your attention to the presence or absence of images. Sit and watch for mental images. These are products of the imagination, recollected from the past or imagined future scenes, or simply made up. Let the images come and go without trying to do anything with them, as if you are interested in what you see but not invested one way or the other in what shows itself. Just sit back and watch the show.

After five or ten minutes, turn your attention to the space in your body in which feelings are registered. Look for any bodily sensations that have an emotional flavoring. These can be obvious feelings or more subtle ones. You may find a hint of sadness, elation, or annoyance in your body. You may find it difficult to distinguish between bodily sensations with and without an emotional flavor. Don't get hung up on doing this precisely. Over time, you will refine your ability to differentiate physical from emotional sensations. Here, too, the pull of stories is great. Just try to see the feelings like the waves on the shore. They come in and they recede; they come in different intensities. Here, too, just feel the movement of feelings as if you were wading in the surf at the edge of the ocean. Try to stay out of the storylines of the feelings, and when you do get pulled in, gently extricate yourself to move back to the energy of the feelings as a phenomenon happening right here and now. Continue observing feelings for five or ten minutes.

Now, let go of any particular focus and bring attention to whatever is happening, whether thought, image, or emotion (or any combination of these); bodily sensation, seeing, hearing, smell, or taste. Meet each experience as it arises. Observe it as it fades away or is replaced by something else. Experience the pageant with a bemused delight and again without any investment in it going any particular way. Do this for five or ten minutes or as long as you like.

Remember that you can return your attention here whenever you can remember to do so. Acknowledge the effort you have just made exploring your experience.

Meditation Reflection

Take a few moments to reflect on what came up for you during this practice. You have taken a tour of your mind. What was most fascinating about this tour? What was most frustrating, confusing, or disappointing? With awareness, were you able to experience thoughts, emotions, and images as objects of your attention?

_____

_____

_____

_____

The QUIET Technique: Your Quick and Portable Mindfulness Companion

Given the mind's tendency to be active and reactive to stimulation, you can benefit from a quick and easy way to bring yourself back to the present. QUIET is an acronym for a technique that helps you quiet your mind in any given moment. This series of five steps is designed to interrupt automatic mind patterns that give rise to distress. It is easy to learn and quick to practice. It only takes a few seconds and one cycle of breathing to do it. You can do the QUIET technique multiple times each day, however many times is necessary until it becomes a beneficial habit.

Q is for *quit*. When you feel distress, *quit* what you are doing. If you are ruminating on the past, stop. If you are complaining about what is happening, disentangle yourself from that bit of internal dialog. If you are involved in a difficult conversation with another person and strong emotions arise, see if you can pause from the conversation for a moment.

U is for *understand* what is happening. *Understand* that there is a connection between what is happening internally or externally and how you feel. You are observing the connection between body and mind in action. You can feel the downstream effects of your thoughts on your body. For instance, anticipating the future gives rise to tension, anxiety, or excitement. The understanding generated here can be a quick affirmation and does not need to be a long, ponderous affair. It is more like an "aha" moment or a quick flash of insight and recognition. The understanding may be generic: *My mind was in the DMN and I am now feeling distressed.* Understanding can also be specific to the particular contents of the DMN in that moment. There are the usual suspects, patterns that occur over and over: themes of insecurity, betrayal, disappointment, doubt, fear of rejection, wanting to impress others, and so forth. It's better to keep your focus on the generic process and not get caught up in the details. The pattern of reactivity may be familiar. For example, you may have caught yourself in the act of beating yourself up for some perceived transgression and you now feel the emotional effects of that flogging. The more you *understand* these connections, the easier it will be to *quit* them.

I is for *inhale*.

E is for *exhale*. Make one cycle of breathing with mindfulness. Reconnect to your body in this moment.

T is for *transition*. Make your *transition* into the next moment with the presence and insight gained from doing the previous steps.

Repeat the process as needed—which will likely be often!

Here's an example of QUIET in action. You are rushing through your day and you notice that you are feeling tense. Your heart pounds, your mouth is dry, and you've got butterflies in your stomach. You also notice that these sensations are accompanied, perhaps even fueled, by a negative anticipation of the future: *I can't get it all done on time*. Noticing these sensations and thoughts gives you the opportunity to "quit." You "understand" how this reaching into the future gives rise to your discomfort. Then you take a mindful cycle of breath: "inhale" and "exhale." Now you can transition to the next moment. You decide to bring your attention from the future to the present, and focus on the task at hand rather than projecting yourself into the future. This gives your nervous system a brief respite and the physiological sensations of heart pounding, dry mouth, and butterflies in the stomach will subside. You can now rest into the present moment.

The result of the QUIET technique is a moment of quiet that ushers in the next moment, breaking the cycle of thinking that can give rise to distress. It takes only a few seconds to do this technique, so you can do it frequently throughout the day. Any time that you notice a change in your state from pleasant to unpleasant, you can get QUIET.

The QUIET technique might be especially useful when you find yourself getting interrupted a lot. These interruptions can be particularly vexing, so we'll explore them in the next section.

Handling Interruptions

Interruptions are the bane of introverts. You may be deeply engaged with an activity, applying your powers of concentration, when someone (likely an extrovert) disturbs you with a question. If it is a nonurgent question, it likely perturbs you. Interruptions are expensive for you in time and energy. It will take time and effort to reengage with your task and you've spent precious energy interacting with the interrupter. Extroverts, by contrast, thrive on multitasking and don't mind interruptions because interruptions add stimulation to their lives.

You already have some familiarity with responding to interruptions that has come through your meditation practice. Each time you retrieve your attention from the storytelling mind of the DMN, you are responding to an interruption. The talking mind interrupts the pure attention of mindfulness and, as you have no doubt discovered, this can happen countless times during any meditation session. The instruction is to return your attention to your breathing or other object of focus and resume practice. The invitation is to make this transition without acrimony, judgment, or resistance. You are encouraged to make this transition in as matter-of-fact way as possible. It's not a big deal unless you make it one. How these interruptions are handled distinguishes expert from novice practitioners. Experts still have minds that interrupt the flow of mindful attention. They are, however, more efficient at returning their attention to the present moment. No big deal. Novices tend to get hung up on the interruption and react to that. When this happens, they have the interruption itself and the reaction to the interruption pushing them further from the present moment. The expert's approach in meditation can also be a model for handling interruptions in the real world.

When you are working and are interrupted—either from within or, more likely, from without—can you use the expert's strategy of returning attention to the present moment as if it is no big deal? Your tendency may be to react, to say to yourself, *Aarrgh, I can't believe she interrupted me and for such a stupid reason. This has ruined my concentration...my morning...my entire day!* That commentary adds extra stress to the situation. Instead, you can try to pick up your attention and return it to the task at hand—just as if you were picking up your attention and returning it to your breath during meditation. No big deal. There are consequences to the interruption (your train of thought has been broken), and there can be further consequences if you have an internal reaction to the interruption—in other words, generating a story about how frustrating, unfair, and unfortunate this interruption is. You can minimize this compounded consequence by training your attention away from the stories you tell yourself so as to return it to reestablishing your concentration on the task at hand.

Another helpful strategy is to proactively preempt interruptions. You can do this by devising a signaling system that you present to coworkers, family members, and perhaps even to your own mind.

Signal Your Availability

You can support your work and personal environments by signaling to the people around you how open you are to interruptions. Take an image from a Caribbean beach where different colored flags signal the condition of the water and how safe it is for swimming. A green flag announces that the waters are calm; you are in a place where you don't mind being interrupted. A yellow flag signals more turbulent waters and to "swim with caution." Your yellow flag tells people that you would rather not be disturbed, but if something important comes up, you can be interrupted. A red flag says, "Not safe to swim!" Similarly, your red flag shouts, "Do not disturb under any circumstances! Unless the building is on fire or someone is bleeding to death, do not interrupt me or you'll experience my wrath!" The system requires a visual signal for communicating your status to others and, of course, a briefing on how the system works and that you are putting it in place. You can use different colored objects or make signs with the different colors. Be creative and have fun with this.

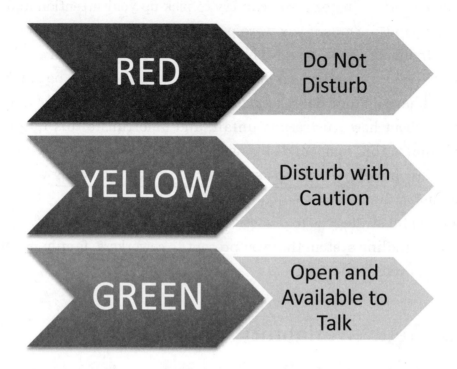

Even with the best signaling system, you will sometimes be disturbed when you don't want to be. The table provided (and available for download online at http://www.newharbinger.com/36101) can help you to monitor the interruptions you experience and track your ability to reengage your attention. For each situation, note the time and, briefly, the circumstances. How long does the interruption go on? Note your feelings and anything you notice in the transition back to your task. Look for any patterns that emerge.

Interruption Monitor

Time	Circumstance	Duration	Feelings	Transition

Are there particular times of day when disruptions are more likely and when it's harder for you to reestablish concentration? What are the feelings that arise? Does your storytelling mind get involved? How does your transition back to the task go? Is it a big, hairy deal, or can it be just the next moment?

_____

_____

_____

Mary's Story: Finding Balance Between the Extremes

Mary is a well-adjusted introvert who practices mindfulness. She experiences the "real" world (where most people are) as a pulsing energy ball. Because she is an introvert, she makes a conscious choice not to live with everyone else at the center of this energy ball; but she also does not want to live in the "outer reaches," which would put her on the fringes of society. Since she cannot tolerate either place—the center of the energy ball or the fringes of society— she lives instead in what might be called the "fluid," between the ball and its orbiting satellites of the outer reaches. Mindfulness functions as a filter that buffers the draining effects of the energy ball. In order to go into the teeming place where most people are, Mary needs a protective bubble or she, as she puts it, "won't be able to survive the real world." Mindfulness practice has helped to make this bubble more robust, durable, and effective.

Mary uses mindfulness to help her to be intentional. She takes a mindful breath before responding to a comment, question, or e-mail. This reflective pause helps her to keep things on track and to avoid interactions moving in directions she does not want them to go. Breathing gives her time to process information. Meditation practice during the course of her workday also helps her to process the social energies from the day and release them before making her transition to home.

Mary aims for a regular practice of mindfulness and sits a few days per week. She can detect a palpable difference when she doesn't practice. She feels more scattered, and after a while, she starts to miss the practice. "Meditation feels like a gift to myself," she says. Without practice, she doesn't feel grounded enough. There was a long period when she didn't meditate, and she found herself reacting more quickly to people and situations. Even ten minutes of practice can help, because it helps her to conserve precious energy that tends to get drained in social situations.

Handling Overstimulation

The earlier part of this chapter documented the differences between the introvert and extrovert brains. Your brain is likely already more active than an extrovert's brain. You don't need lots of excitement to get you going. In fact, such stimulation can readily become overwhelming. The noisy, chaotic, and high-intensity world can be a challenge. What can you do to cope, especially if you have to work in one of these environments, such as an open-plan office? (According to Kim and de Dear [2013], the open-plan office is known to be a stressful environment, especially for introverts.)

Mindfulness, of course, can be a staple of your survival plan. When you can bring an open curiosity to the environment around you, it is possible to be mindful in a noisy train station as well as a quiet cave. Acceptance is key. Tension arises when there is resistance to the sounds, energy, and commotion. It is as if your mind is saying, *This shouldn't be happening; I can't tolerate this.* Despite your protests, the reality of the situation is what it is, and that reality gives rise to stress and tension when you resist it. Just as you have done with the body scan, you can do an "environment scan," bringing your attention—with interest, curiosity, even fascination—to whatever is happening around you. You can imagine that you are a scientist from another world sent to this place to document the setting. If you look out over the open office, for example, you will see and hear a variety of things: people talking, moving, and working; phones ringing, machines whirring, and fingers typing. It can be a nightmare of stress, or a symphonic ballet of movement and sound—your attitude makes all the difference. Acceptance is a general strategy to adopt, but it is easier to tell you to accept your environment than it is to actually do it, especially if you need to overcome a lifetime of conditioning that taught you to react negatively to environments like these. Practice will be the key to making this transition.

Regular mindfulness practice in your office or other stressful situations can help. I call this "executive meditation," and it consists of scheduling a few minutes of every hour for a formal practice. You can use your scheduling technology, such as Outlook or another electronic calendar, to leave yourself reminders to take three to five minutes each hour to pause and pay attention to your breathing and body. Perhaps you'll notice all the tension you've accumulated over the past hour. This brief practice will interrupt that stress process and help you get back to a more relaxed place. Each time you practice, you are training yourself to be resilient to the stresses around you. You can also practice before you enter the stressful situation and again afterward. This can help you to inoculate yourself to the stimulation to come and help you to process through any residue once the experience is over. Think, for example, about diamonds. A diamond is nothing more than a hunk of coal that performed well under pressure. Mindfulness can help you to transform the lumps of coal in your life into diamonds.

Concluding Thoughts

Mindfulness requires paying attention to what is happening in the moment, and to pay attention fully there must be an absence of resistance to what is happening. Can you be fully present without any inner commentary, without any opinions, and without any agenda? In other words, can you adopt a posture of acceptance? When mindfulness and acceptance are both present, you can make the most of what is happening now. In fact, one definition of mindfulness could be this attitude of acceptance. When you can break the habit of the mind's incessant questioning, you can enter into a place of acceptance.

Introversion brings its own challenges for acceptance. Can you accept that you are different from extroverts? Can you accept that you are outside of the extrovert mainstream? While this may be inconvenient at times, it is your truth.

Acceptance opens your mind to the reality of now. Acceptance conserves energy because you are not pushing against this reality. You can rest in the moment.

Chapter 8

Happiness the Introvert Way

Our first task in this chapter is to explore the proposition that extroverts are happier than introverts. Current research definitions of happiness conform to the mainstream ideal of extroversion and overlook happiness as considered from an introvert perspective. There are other ways to look at happiness—ones that are in harmony with your introvert way of being in the world. We will also look at the important experiences of gratitude and vulnerability. Gratitude is a robust antidote to the things that get in the way of your happiness, particularly when you find living in the extrovert world vexing. And when it comes to vulnerability, if extroversion glosses over it, introversion embraces it. Exploring vulnerability with an eye toward acceptance can empower you to be yourself regardless of other people's expectations. You are already quite familiar with your emotional landscape and perhaps have a sense that happiness requires both gratitude and vulnerability. In this chapter, you'll learn how to use mindfulness to refine this familiarity with exercises for learning how to navigate this inner environment more skillfully.

Are Extroverts Happier?

Our culture tells us, "Be extroverted." After all, extroverts allegedly have all the fun at the best parties, while the introverts are bunkered in at home on a Friday night. You have probably run into that caricature when you just wanted to go home after a draining week at work to enjoy some quiet time, whatever that might mean for you. The culture has made extrovert ideals of "fun" a proxy for happiness. Much of the research on introversion and extroversion seems to confirm that extroversion is the way to happiness (Lucas and Fujita 2000). However, this is really not the case. Your introvert way of being happy is just not captured by the way mainstream research is conducted. For example, happiness is defined narrowly as a boisterous, outgoing energy that naturally looks like extroversion. Missing is a quieter, low-impact form of happiness that grows out of peace, tranquillity, and ease.

One recent study highlights the cultural and scientific bias concerning extroverts and introverts. Zelenski, Santoro, and Whelan (2012) conducted research where they measured personality and then asked participants to act like either extroverts or introverts. To act "extroverted," participants "were instructed to act bold, talkative, energetic, active, assertive, and adventurous." To act "introverted," participants "were asked to act reserved, quiet, lethargic, passive, compliant, and unadventurous." Not surprisingly, the results of the study found that both introverts and extroverts felt better when they followed the extrovert instructions. It seems self-evident that anyone asked to act *lethargic* will feel worse than someone who is asked to act *energetic*, and that is what this study found. The take-home message from this study is that brief periods of acting exuberant can feel good, no matter who you are. This is no secret, as you have probably experienced this many times in your life. The study's introverts did not feel drained by acting like extroverts. However, the brief, twenty-minute, experimental periods were not long enough to measure whether this acting comes with an energetic cost to introverts. You probably know from your own experience that prolonged acting like an extrovert *is* taxing.

Hills and Argyle (2001) are some of the few researchers to identify the anti-introvert bias present in research. They lament, "The view that extroversion is a preferred state has come to be widely accepted among social psychologists. In consequence, introverts are sometimes represented as withdrawn, isolated, or lacking social competence, rather than as individuals who seek independence and autonomy" (597). Indeed, the connection between the sociable extrovert and happiness may just reflect the culture's prevailing tendency toward this gregarious way of being. Such gregarious sociability was not in favor in the ancient Greece of Aristotle and Epicurus. Both Aristotle and Epicurus advocated a thoughtful, introspective life in relative solitude away from the masses—an introverted ideal that is lost in our popular culture today. Nor was the contemporary view of extroversion favored during the time of the Buddha in ancient India, where he advocated an introverted path of looking within.

Zelenski and his colleagues did another study (2013) and found that introverts may underestimate the benefits of acting bold. In other words, they make a prediction error that the foray into extroversion won't be fun and pleasurable but negative and self-conscious. If not for this error, the researchers surmised, introverts might enjoy acting extroverted more frequently. The introverts in the study actually did enjoy acting like extroverts for the same twenty-minute period as in the Zelenski, Santoro, and Whelan (2012) experiment.

Zelenski and colleagues (2013) conclude, "It seems most people enjoy behaving in extraverted ways more than behaving in introverted ways" (1093). This appears to be a solid endorsement for the benefits of being an extrovert. If this were true, however, it would lend credibility to the cultural notion that you should just try harder to be more like an extrovert. As with the earlier study, it seems clear that people in these studies are happier simply because they are acting happier; it may have nothing to do with their personality. The study found something very interesting, but because of the biases in research and the culture at large, the researchers described the study's subjects in a way that promoted extroversion rather than the behaviors that produced happiness.

Despite this bias, it might be interesting to try the Zelenski experiment of acting happier (just don't call it extroversion). You may well be familiar with this phenomenon. You are invited to an event and you dread going. You make a negative appraisal of what it will be like. Because of a friend, a spouse, or just by the sheer force of your own will, you are persuaded to go to the event. You wind up having a wonderful time. You are still drained by this event, but surprised that you enjoyed yourself so much.

Act "Bold, Talkative, Energetic, Adventurous, and Assertive": An Experiment for Introverts

The Zelenski studies suggest that introverts are bad at making predictions. What would happen if you *did* force yourself to act in these ways even when you didn't feel like doing it? Zelenski and colleagues (2013) wrote, "We feel confident in suggesting to our introverted readers that a few more moments of extraverted behavior might be good for their happiness (even if they do not think so)" (1106).

Try the Zelenski experiment: spend twenty minutes acting "bold, talkative, energetic, active, assertive, and adventurous." Since the experiment was done in groups, try to do this in a group setting.

How did you feel immediately after the experiment?

_____

_____

_____

_____

How did you feel hours after the experiment?

_____

_____

_____

_____

Expand Your Range

Now that you've tried the Zelenski experiment, you can look for other opportunities to apply what you've learned. You can try to expand the range of situations where you have at least a modicum of comfort; you will grow that comfort the more you challenge yourself.

Where are the safe situations in your life where you can experiment with trying something improvisational? Who are the people with whom you can do this? Is it with your closest friends? Perhaps you might consider playing a game of charades, singing karaoke, or doing something else that typically resides outside of your comfort zone. Brainstorm some possible ideas:

_____

_____

_____

_____

In any given situation, it can be hard to know whether to push yourself or to take care of yourself by staying in your comfort zone. Answering the question "What's the best way to take care of myself in this moment?" can be difficult. The following meditation can help you to figure out the best way to take care of yourself in the situations that you confront.

Formal Practice: *The "Know Thyself, Respect Thyself, Push Thyself" Contemplation*

How can you tell the difference between cases of accurately or inaccurately forecasting how you will enjoy an event? Try this exercise.

Get into your meditation posture. Settle into your breath and body for a couple of minutes. Bring to mind an image of the event that you are considering going to. Try to imagine the event in great detail. If you've been to this place before, you can fill in the details quite readily. If you haven't, create the details using your imagination. As you sit with this image, notice what feelings come into your body. Bring your attention to these feelings and keep breathing. Ask yourself, Can I open myself to this environment? Where is my energy right now? Is it important for me to go to this event? Does it connect with my core values?

Can you remember going to a similar event? If so, remember how you actually felt. Which part of the event left the biggest impression? Was it the dread of going? Was there a sweet spot during the event where you really began to enjoy yourself? Did you need a warm-up period to get to this point? As you pose these questions, notice if there is any change in your energy. A feeling of spaciousness may indicate a green light for the event. A feeling of dread that persists may indicate a red or at least a yellow light.

Meditation Reflection

Take a few moments to consider this practice. Were you able to notice changes in your energy? How does it feel to open to these situations with the practice of mindfulness?

_____

_____

_____

_____

Tapping into your feelings will not give you definite answers, but it can help you to collect some useful information. This contemplation can help you to draw the line between skillful self-care (that is, you really need to rest and restore because you've had a taxing week at work) and mistaken forecasting (that is, you just don't feel like going because you think it's going to be a drag). It will take experience (that is, experimenting with going and not going) and self-knowledge (cultivated through mindfulness) to differentiate between skillful self-care and mistaken forecasting. Making that differentiation is not an exact science, but unless you push your boundary once in a while, you won't know where your boundary really is. You can find that boundary, that frontier between the known and comfortable and the unknown and uncertain. If you push yourself relentlessly through that boundary, consider being gentler. If your tendency is always to shy away, consider giving yourself a little push once in a while to see how that feels.

Acting extroverted is similar to *behavioral activation*, an approach that has been used to treat depression and has been found to be an effective way to increase subjective well-being (Mazzucchelli, Kane, and Rees 2010). Acting *as if* you are happy can actually move you toward being happy. Similar results have been found with smiling. Even forcing a smile can lead to an increase in positive feelings (Strack, Martin, and Stepper 1988). Behavioral activation is best accomplished by activities that are enjoyable and consistent with your values. The next section will guide you through experiments that will help you build the skill of distinguishing the occasions when you need to hold back and those when you can push yourself.

The Introvert Actuary

An actuary calculates risks, among other things, and in your own life you are often called upon to make actuarial predictions about your enjoyment of future events. How accurate are you at making these predictions? Look at your social calendar for the upcoming month. List the events on the form that follows. (Additional copies of the form, if you need them, are available online at http://www.newharbin ger.com/36101.) Then estimate your predicted enjoyment of each event on a scale from 1 to 10, with 1 being the worst time you could ever imagine and 10 being the best time you could imagine (compared to the best time you've ever had). After the event, indicate your actual enjoyment, again using the scale of 1 to 10, with 1 being the worst time and 10 being the best time.

Predicted vs. Actual Enjoyment

Social Event	Predicted Enjoyment	Actual Enjoyment

Was there a discrepancy between your predicted and actual enjoyment of these events? How do you understand that discrepancy? Does this discrepancy help you to move your comfort line, or does it confirm that your current boundary is where it should be?

_____

_____

_____

_____

_____

_____

Now that we've explored predicting the enjoyment of situations and experimenting with expanding your range, we can now look at the question of happiness itself.

Uncoupling Happiness from Introversion and Extroversion

As previously stated, happiness is often associated with extroversion in the popular imagination, usually in the form of high-intensity and high-frequency socializing. Yet these exuberant social contacts are not the only source of happiness. The happy introvert can find happiness in solitude and a less intense social calendar.

Indeed, Hills and Argyle (2001) found that variables related to life satisfaction and fulfillment matter more for the generation of happiness than extroversion does, regardless of your personality type. In other words, being highly sociable in extrovert style does not always lead to happiness. What matters most is not how introverted or extroverted you are, but how you live your life. Finding meaning, significance, and connection in your life is what is most important, and this does not have to conform to the extrovert norm. In the Hills and Argyle study, the happy introverts were not just richer in the personality trait of emotional stability—in other words, how neurotic or high-strung they were, or weren't. They had found their own way to happiness. This study also counters the popular image of introverts as bookworms. The happy extroverts actually read more than happy introverts!

Research shows that introverts enjoy socializing as much as extroverts, and they have equivalent social skills. The research subject introvert, often a college student, does not necessarily look the same as the real-world introvert. Zelenski, Sobocko, and Whelan (2014) make the important point that "most people are happy most of the time" (192). Even when happiness is measured in conventional extrovert-centered ways, most studies find that extroverts are just slightly happier than introverts; this does not mean that the introverts in these studies were unhappy, just slightly less happy than the extroverts. Also, such differences may be statistically significant, but whether they make a difference in the real world is unclear. Other factors of personality (such as neuroticism or emotional stability) influence happiness to a greater extent.

A New Way of Defining Happiness

Extroverts need high levels of stimulation to feel good (supplied by the neurotransmitter dopamine), whereas introverts can feel good at low levels of stimulation (because they already have high levels of dopamine). These high-stimulation pleasant states have come to be seen as the benchmark of happiness. Zelenski and colleagues (2013) affirm something that you have probably noticed in your own experience. The reason that you are not motivated to pursue pleasurable activities to the same extent as the extroverts in your life is that you often already find yourself in a pleasant state. In research, feelings are often measured by the Positive and Negative Affect Scale (PANAS). The PANAS sees positive emotions as pleasant *and* aroused—for example, "enthusiastic, excited, alert." Zelenski, Sobocko, and Whelan (2014) point out, "If happiness questionnaires assess only the exuberance of parties rather than the contentment of quiet walks, they would be biased to a more extraverted form of happiness" (187). Of course, you and all other introverts want to be happy. You just don't want the extroverted form of happiness. When given the choice, introverts prefer less stimulating emotions (Rusting and Larsen 1997). An introvert's view of feelings does not appear on the PANAS. Introvert author Sophia Dembling (2012) provides a list of low-arousal, less stimulating (or what we'll call "introvert-style") positive feelings: "peaceful, content, engaged, engrossed, focused, amused, composed, calm" (79). To this list you can add delight, equanimity, tranquillity, serenity, and bliss. These low-arousal feelings expand the concept of happiness.

In Praise of Introvert-Style Positive Feelings

In this section is a list of introvert-style positive feelings. For each feeling, reflect on your life and write about a situation where you felt this feeling.

Introvert-Style Positive Feelings

Feeling	Description
Bemused	
Calm	
Contented	
Engaged	
Engrossed	
Serene	
Tranquil	
Other	

How can you increase the frequency of the situations that give rise to these feelings?

_____

_____

_____

_____

Introverts get their rewards from lower-key activities and don't need all the hustle and bustle that extroverts thrive on. What are the activities that you enjoy the most?

_____

_____

_____

How often do you do these activities? Are other people involved?

_____

_____

_____

If you found that this exercise revealed that you don't spend enough time in activities that give rise to introvert-style, low-stimulation pleasant feelings, you can now put these on your radar screen. If you are already spending time with these activities then you can reaffirm their importance in your life and look for additional opportunities to integrate them into your life. In the next section, you can look more closely at the relationship between your behaviors and your values.

Aligning Your Actions and Values

The Zelenski studies (2012, 2013) did not do a follow-up beyond the lab period to see if there were energetic costs for the introverts who acted extroverted. The time spent extroverting was also of short duration (only twenty minutes). There may be longer-term costs to acting against your disposition. McGregor, McAdams, and Little (2006) pointed out that self-knowledge must include an awareness of personality traits, and that an authentic life should have goals that are consistent with that personality. When there is a mismatch between one's goals and personality, frustration, stress, and unhappiness may result. Here McGregor and colleagues consider the dilemma facing college students: "Imagine a highly introverted individual committed to an identity and a set of goals related to becoming a 'party animal.' Because introvert neurophysiology is easily overwhelmed by high levels of stimulation, being a party animal could be particularly challenging and aversive for the introvert" (553).

The energy required for this introverted "party animal" aspirant would be great, draining energy away from other important aspects of life. In addition, the stimulation may feel overwhelming and even make it difficult to be that party animal. It's a lose-lose situation for this introvert.

While it may be expeditious on occasion to act counter to your introvert disposition, a long-term strategy of doing this is likely to be counterproductive. Students were happiest when they were extroverted *and* valued sociability *and* engaged in high levels of social activities. While introverts may wish to be more like party animal extroverts, it is unlikely to be a path to enduring happiness.

Because of the pitfalls of being an introvert in an extrovert culture, you can benefit from a more deliberate consideration of your life, which we will explore in the following section. This vision can help you to spend your time acting in ways that are going to nurture you in the long run.

Creating Your Vision of Life: Embracing Your Truth

The best way to embrace your truth and live the life that is most fulfilling to you is to create a vision for your life that is grounded in your introvert strengths. Contemplate the vision you'd like to see for your life. Fill in the who, what, when, where, and why for this vision.

When you envision the life that would make you the happiest and have the most pleasure, meaning, and significance, what are you doing in your work and personal life?

_____

_____

_____

_____

_____

_____

_____

Where is this taking place? What are the settings and artistic features of this place? Is the environment quiet? How is chaos managed?

_____

_____

_____

_____

_____

_____

Why is this vision of life important to you? What personal values are you tapping into?

_____

_____

_____

_____

_____

_____

Who is with you on this journey? What role do others play in your vision? How much time is spent in solitude versus connecting with others?

_____

_____

_____

_____

_____

_____

When does this vision take place? What needs to happen before you can make it a reality?

_____

_____

_____

_____

_____

_____

What steps can you take today to move toward your vision? These steps may be practical or internal.

_____

_____

_____

_____

Sometimes it is critical to give yourself permission to put your values first, before the needs of others or their expectations for you as an introvert. Can you make this a priority? How will you make it a priority?

_____

_____

_____

_____

Coordinate these thoughts into a description of your vision. The more consistent your vision is with your introvert tendencies, the more satisfying this vision of life will be. For instance, you may tap into something that you have always wanted to do but haven't been able to give yourself permission to pursue. Perhaps it is a life of serving others, or the pursuit of a hidden talent such as music, art, or sport. Can you articulate a preliminary statement of this vision?

_____

_____

_____

_____

Constructing the vision for your life is bound to bring you into close contact with the things you are most grateful for. In turn, a consideration of gratitude can help to inform the vision of your life.

Gratitude

A feeling of gratitude can be a potent antidote to negativity in any moment. Gratitude is a staple of positive psychology—the study of what makes us feel good and perform our best (Ben-Shahar 2007). While there are almost always valid negative things to focus on in any situation, gratitude practice recognizes the wisdom of emphasizing what is positive rather than dwelling on problems. As an introvert, you may be prone to getting sucked into the problems you have to face: the loud extroverts who don't understand you, the lack of privacy in your office, the hectic pace of life. It's easy to get sucked into these particular stories. Gratitude doesn't deny that these problems are real and need to be addressed. Instead, the focus shifts to the things that are going right in your life. An emphasis on gratitude can help to maintain a positive perspective and counteract the sometime introvert tendency to ruminate and focus on the negative.

Gratitude List

For today, what are you most grateful for? If you're having a difficult day, don't forget the basics like being alive, having enough to eat, and having loved ones. There is *always* something to be grateful for. Just having the opportunity to sit and breathe can be a source for gratitude.

Today's Gratitude List

_____

_____

_____

_____

Working Gratitude List (What are some enduring things you are grateful for?)

_____

_____

_____

Introvert Gratitude List (What are the things you value most about being an introvert?)

_____

_____

_____

_____

_____

Lucinda's Story: What's Not Wrong

Lucinda, an introvert, meets every Wednesday night with a group of friends at the same Italian restaurant (lasagna is the Wednesday night special). She and her friends go around the table and respond to the question "What's the best thing that happened to you today?" Such a start to the evening, no doubt, prevents a descent into grousing, complaining, and other forms of negativity. One evening in February, when it was Lucinda's turn to speak, she said, "When I fell through the ice, I didn't go all the way under." Earlier that day, she was ice-skating on Vermont's frozen Lake Champlain. It was a typical sunny, twenty-degree February day. The ice gave way and she fell in, but somehow she didn't get submerged. She was able to grab on to the remaining ice and extricate herself before making a chilly return to shore. Recounting that day, she said, "I could have complained about falling through the ice and the uncomfortable hypothermia that resulted, yet I decided to emphasize something positive about the experience and to make it humorous. I was truly grateful that I didn't go under the water. It could have been much worse." As it turned out, one of her friends in the group had been out taking pictures that day, and he gave her a composite of photographs producing a panoramic view of the lake, including the spot where Lucinda fell in. Lucinda still looks at that picture with pleasure each time she sees it hanging in her home, instead of dwelling in anxiety over what happened (or what could have happened). Gratitude helped her to put this experience in a different context. Lucinda recommends gratitude practice to everyone she meets. As she puts it, "It can be good to start your day with gratitude as well as to end it with gratitude."

Embracing Vulnerability

An increased awareness of gratitude helps to bring into focus what is most precious. And with that awareness comes the recognition that we are vulnerable to loss and change. Like introversion, vulnerability has gotten a bad reputation in our culture—and this is no coincidence. Part of the allure of this culture of extroversion is a sense of invulnerability, that can-do attitude that refuses to stop or say no. There is no room for vulnerability. It is seen as weakness. Consider the financial crisis of 2007–2008 and its fallout in the following years. A vocal minority made reckless decisions that led to the financial collapse. A sense of invulnerability characterized the rise to the financial crisis. A greater sense of vulnerability would have led to caution and a more heedful approach to decision making and risk taking.

Vulnerability includes what Mark Epstein (2013) calls the "trauma of everyday life." There is no escape from sickness, aging, and eventual death. Every moment is beset with the potential for losing something that we want or gaining something that we don't want. We cannot control much of what happens to us. If we deny all this, we are cut off from reality and waste a lot of energy denying and struggling against that reality.

Embracing vulnerability requires an acceptance of imperfection. Vulnerability is not weakness, as the work of Brené Brown (2010) makes so poignant. As Brown writes, "Owning our story can be hard but not nearly as difficult as spending our lives running from it. Embracing our vulnerabilities is risky but not nearly as dangerous as giving up on love and belonging and joy—the experiences that make us the most vulnerable. Only when we are brave enough to explore the darkness will we discover the infinite power of our light" (6). Being an introvert can be risky business. Asking for what you need from extroverts (and introverts who have not yet declared their independence from the culture of extroversion) makes you vulnerable to criticism, pity, and misunderstanding. It's easier to comply with the groupthink, but when you do this, something important is lost—like joy and a sense of belonging, or even love, as Brown suggests. It sometimes takes courage to say no to the invitation that will overtax your energy. Likewise, it takes courage to go to a wearing event when it is important to you or someone close to you. It sometimes takes daring to educate the people around you that introverts are not misfits, misanthropes, and malcontents. It sometimes requires valor to be silent because you are not ready to speak, especially when the people around you are comfortable shooting from the hip with half-formed ideas. It takes guts to explore your interior with meditation. Author and poet David Whyte (2009) speaks of the myth of perfectionism and invulnerability. Our culture says that power, accomplishment, and value come from a place of inviolability. Whyte points out that this is a myth: "If I spend any time in silence, any time watching the way my mind works, I will find that there is a way in which we withhold the very thing from ourselves that might provide us with the possibility of happiness. What we withhold from ourselves is the willingness to understand our own imperfection. The strategic, intellectual self, looking in from the outside, cannot have the experience of sheer physical vulnerability that the deeper internal self must gain to walk through the door of self-compassion" (304).

Whyte points out that we become whole by embracing our vulnerabilities. The very doorway to that wholeness is vulnerability, an admission of imperfection and the inability to be present at every moment, even when we are committed to mindfulness. Vulnerability is not knowing all the answers; it is not being able to be "on" all the time. It is not having boundless energy. It is being sensitive to conditions. It is a yearning for silence in the unrelenting tumult.

If you stopped pretending to be perfect, inviolate, and impeccable 100 percent of the time, what would you like to say about your life in this moment? For instance, you could admit that you have doubts, you could confess that you are tired, you could relax into this moment without having to make an impression on someone else.

_____

_____

_____

_____

_____

What would you say if you could embrace your sense of vulnerability and speak your truth without fear of judgment, recrimination, or censure (from yourself or others)?

_____

_____

_____

_____

_____

Concluding Thoughts

This chapter has looked at the happiness side of emotional life from the introvert's perspective. Relish your greater sense of flexibility for defining happiness and your deepened appreciation for low-stimulation, introvert-style pleasurable feelings such as tranquillity and calm. Ample mindfulness practice in combination with proactive strategies, such as expressing gratitude and acknowledging vulnerability, can keep you aimed toward happiness.

Chapter 9

The Buddha Was
an Introvert

The story of a privileged kid, Siddhartha Gautama, who became the Buddha can show you a path from pretending to be an extrovert to embracing the value of introversion. Despite living twenty-five hundred years ago, the Buddha's story has a lesson for introverts living today because it appears that he was an introvert who lived much of his earlier life conforming to extrovert expectations. Yet he found a way to move beyond these expectations and embrace an introverted view and approach to life that resulted in profound peace, wisdom, and happiness.

Much of what is known about the Buddha's biography comes from a handful of cryptic statements he made in his teachings. Often referred to as a prince, he was born into a life of ease, and in one of his lectures he gives a glimpse of what this courtly life was like. He had separate houses for the seasons, and he was constantly entertained. In the Anguttara Sutra, the Buddha said, "I lived in refinement, utmost refinement, total refinement... A white sunshade was held over me day and night to protect me from cold, heat, dust, dirt, and dew... During the four months of the rainy season, I was entertained in the rainy season palace by minstrels without a single man among them" (Bhikku 1996, 1).

Sounds like an extrovert-style party! The young prince lived a life of luxury, pampering, and amusement. He likely had no privacy as he was constantly engaged in courtly functions, games, and the care of his royal person. This would have been a challenging life for an introvert. One exceptional moment of privacy occurred when Siddhartha was eight years old. He separated himself from the group celebrating the harvest, sat under a rose apple tree, and went into spontaneous meditation. This event was an early sign of his introvert and spiritual leanings. We know that despite his advantage, Siddhartha was not happy. If Siddhartha was an introvert, as his time under the rose apple tree and his later life suggest, then he must have spent much of his early life pretending or being forced to be an extrovert. This, no doubt, contributed to his sense of dissatisfaction with life. After twenty-nine years, he left his home to seek a more enduring happiness.

The story of the Buddha's life is more allegory than literal truth. The reader is asked to accept that he had not seen a sick, old, or dead person until he was twenty-nine. This would seem to be a physical impossibility. However, according to the legend, his sudden exposure to these "signs" provoked a crisis that inspired him to seek a deeper meaning to life for himself and for others as well. The sight of a sick man, an old man, and a dead man shook Siddhartha's worldview. He realized how impermanence pervaded everything—especially human life. From then on it made no point to him to blindly pursue pleasure because all of life was fleeting. There had to be a way to escape from the pervasive dissatisfaction that he felt in his own experience and the experience of those around him. He then set out as a wandering yogi, living in the forest for the next six years and practicing extreme privations. He did have a handful of practice companions, but most of the work was done in solitary silence. Despite his prodigious efforts, he did not eradicate that sense of dissatisfaction or shake off his existential crisis. There had to be another way.

After these years of isolated deprivation, the soon-to-be Buddha realized a middle path was needed—something in between an extroverted life of pleasure seeking and a loner ascetic's life of denying the needs of the body. That middle path became his teaching, grounded in mindfulness. The path the Buddha advocated was more weighted toward the introverted side of the continuum—practicing alone and in silence. The Buddha gave these basic instructions in the Majjhima Nikaya 10: "There is the case where a monk—having gone to the wilderness, to the foot of a tree, or to an empty building—sits down folding his legs crosswise, holding his body erect, and setting mindfulness to the fore. Always mindful, he breathes in; mindful, he breathes out" (Bhikku 1996, 236).

Uttiya, one of the followers of the Buddha, aimed for the following aspiration from the Buddha's teachings or *dhamma* (also styled *dharma*) when he said in the Samyutta Nikaya 47, "I might dwell alone, secluded, heedful, ardent, and resolute" (Bikkhu 1996, 82). These qualities sound like a roster of introvert strengths.

The Buddha's Awakening

Going back to the Buddha's story: On the verge of collapse from starvation, Siddhartha abandoned both his path of deprivation and his few ascetic colleagues and accepted a meal from a young cowherd girl. Fortified by this simple meal of rice wrapped in a banana leaf, he sat down under a tree and resolved to not get up until he had found a way beyond the pervasive stress he felt in his life—a stress that appeared to be universal for others as well. When the Buddha sat down under a pipal or fig tree (now known as the bodhi tree), in what is now Bodhgaya, India, he went into a period of intensive meditation. He practiced what we would now call mindfulness meditation. He focused on his breathing and bodily sensations. He saw his thoughts, memories, and emotions come and go. In the midst of these observations, he noticed something profound: everything was constantly changing, including his sense of self. He discovered that this sense of self arises out of all the other mental processes of the mind and does not have an independent existence. However, for the preceding thirty-five years, he had been living his life as if this self *did* have an independent existence, and this mistaken belief was the root cause of all suffering. These insights brought about an awakening. The now Buddha (which simply means "awakened one") realized that the self, while embedded in a personality, is not a solid entity. The self is fluid, impermanent, and malleable. Many yogis had achieved profound states of meditation long before the Buddha, but he was the first yogi to bring a radical cognitive and self-empowering view to the problem of existence.

Buddhist scholar Richard Gombrich (2009) highlights the Buddha's revolutionary insight when he notes, "A great deal of modern education and psychotherapy consists of making people aware that they are responsible for themselves. In fact, we consider that it constitutes a large part of what we mean by becoming a mature person. It is amazing that someone should have promulgated this idea in the fifth century BC, and hardly less remarkable that he found followers" (14) Twenty-five hundred years ago people relied on priests, rituals, and faith-based dogmatic beliefs for their salvation. The Buddha offered a psychological and empirical approach—in other words, an approach that involved looking within for the answers to life's big questions. No beliefs were required, just a willingness to practice. The Buddha's profound insight was that misery is self-inflicted by how mental life is conducted (that's the bad news). Even though anguish is habitually and unconsciously created, it is possible to intervene with this misery-making process through intellectual understanding and a behavioral commitment to change (that's the good news). These behaviors are encompassed within an ethical approach to living life and a dedication to mindfulness.

The Buddha probably did not think in terms of introversion and extroversion because those terms were not in fashion, but he likely did observe that some people were externally focused while others were more interior. Introverts and extroverts will come to the internal work of mindfulness from different starting points but will ultimately wind up in the same place—that is, all will need to transcend the labels of "introvert" and "extrovert." The extrovert must slow down long enough to look within. The introvert must disentangle the mind from self-generated stories long enough to bring attention to what is happening now. It's an over/under problem. The introvert is *over*-interested in the interior while the extrovert is *under*-interested. The introvert gets bogged down in stories and can spend a lot of energy lost in thinking. Life is overshadowed by imagination. Mindfulness helps introverts to reorient to the reality of the present moment.

Regardless of the starting place, the Buddha's teachings apply to everyone, introverts and extroverts alike. His first set of teachings came soon after his awakening under the tree, and these teachings are known as the "four noble truths."

The Four Noble Truths, Introvert-Style

The Buddha's first lesson, contained in the four noble truths, was perhaps his most important and enduring one. These four insights are the ground of his psychology. They are an interrelated set of understandings and actions that can guide every moment of waking life. Mindfulness is an integral component of this practical philosophy.

If the Buddha had given a special sermon to introverts, he would have encouraged introverts to tap into their interior mind connection to aid them on a path toward liberation from suffering. This interior connection is an asset, because it is within the mind that suffering is constructed. This internal access, however, is also a liability when the mind gets too identified with thoughts. The Buddha would have taught introverts to take care of themselves yet discouraged them from becoming too aligned with the contents of their minds. Introverted introspection is the route to liberation. Liberation cannot be achieved through an extroverted approach to life that is noisy, active, and high intensity. But, as I noted above, the introvert's tendency to get bogged down in stories can also thwart liberation. This is why mindfulness is so important.

The middle path is tilted toward the introverted side of things. It is both interior and open to the outer senses. It abides in stillness and in motion, but is rooted in the vast stillness that can be found in sitting practice. The prototypical image is the solitary yogi who sits quietly alone among others who are also practicing in silence. Attention is with the outer and inner phenomena available to consciousness: the five senses, and the subjective components of mind—thoughts, images, and emotions. However, the introverted yogi is attending to the *process* of these internal and external senses, not their contents, meanings, or implications. The extrovert learns to become comfortable in stillness and the introvert learns to let go of these mental contents. That's the challenge—to let go. The stories can be quite compelling and form the foundation of identity. Can you let go?

Letting Go of Thoughts

Sit quietly for five minutes and take note of all the thoughts that present themselves to your attention. Write some of these thoughts down:

_____

_____

_____

_____

What would it be like if you were to let these thoughts go? Does your well-being seem to depend on these thoughts? Who would you be if these thoughts were not true, important, or relevant?

_____

_____

_____

_____

What does your mind seem to be seeking by engaging these thoughts? Is it reassurance, entertainment, or something else?

_____

_____

_____

_____

First Noble Truth: The Truth of Dukkha

The first truth was provoked years ago by Siddhartha's encounter with sickness, old age, and death: life has inescapable suffering. We cannot control loss. No one is immune. The insight then goes deeper. It is not just these big-ticket items that give rise to suffering; there is *something else* that permeates every moment of experience. The first truth is the truth of *dukkha*. The term "dukkha" is often translated as suffering but it is also translated as stress, anguish, misery, or dissatisfaction. The term captures each of these facets of experience, yet dukkha is a metaphor. It literally means "bad wheel," and the Buddha offered the image of an oxcart with a broken wheel. If you ride on the oxcart that represents life, that bad wheel will affect every moment of the journey. The Buddha realized that even when things are going well, there can be an underlying sense of dissatisfaction. We may be afraid of losing what we have, or we may have a gnawing sense that something is off, or not just right. The more he meditated, the more he saw how pervasive this dukkha was.

As an introvert, living in the extroverted world leaves you feeling off, dissatisfied, stressed, and even anguished. Being part of this culture, you face an extra challenge, much like trying to make a square peg fit in a round hole. The introvert-specific version of dukkha exists both at a conscious level and, more importantly, at deeper, unconscious levels. You may not even be aware of all the ways that your introvert qualities are being overlooked, devalued, or denied. You may have been vaguely familiar with this *offness*, even though it was occurring out of awareness.

Reflect on your life in this moment. Think about all the points of dissatisfaction. What keeps you from being happy? Write down the reasons you are unhappy or the things you'd like to change. This is part of your dukkha list.

_____

_____

_____

_____

Second Noble Truth: The Truth of the Cause of Dukkha

The next truth sought to understand and explain the first truth. What causes dissatisfaction? Why are we stressed? The Buddha had a radical insight at this juncture. The recognition of suffering was not particularly novel; religions had focused on it long before him. But the Buddha, in contrast to the religions of his time, did not see suffering as a result of fate or the will of the gods. He saw anguish as self-inflicted. We play a role in creating our experience. Our mental attitudes (including intentions) and the behaviors that stem from these attitudes will make the difference between suffering and peace. The radical idea was that it is not what happens to us that is most important; it is how we relate to what happens to us. The Buddha identified *desire* as the culprit. We want the things that we want and we don't want the things that we don't want. This wanting creates a constant tension of pulling toward or pushing away. It gives rise to what amounts to a background "radiation" of dukkha, an anxiety that we may not get what we want and, consequently, that we will not be okay. It's an energy that is always present although barely perceptible at times.

One major cause of anguish for you as an introvert is the expectation that you conform to the extrovert norms. You may be overwhelmed by noisy, chaotic, open-plan offices, exhausted from superficial social contacts, and distracted by constant interruptions. The introvert-specific version of dukkha arises from your own expectations and those of others about how to conform to the larger norms of the culture. There is an underlying pressure to buy into the extrovert version of happiness: loud, social, and exciting. The cause of this misery is a lack of acceptance. When you want things to be other than they are in the moment, anguish follows. This can take the form of self-judgment: *I should be like the extroverts around me.* This expectation will give rise to a pressure to conform and a mismatch between the reality of what the situation demands and what you have to offer. Accepting your limitations and seeking to take care of yourself in these situations is the alternative to self-condemnation. While you will have to accept your limitations in some areas, you can use your strengths in other areas. A lack of self-care based on either denial or ignorance gives rise to much of your unique introvert-based suffering.

Look at the dukkha list you generated in the exercise on the first noble truth. How would these items change if you were to let go of clinging—that is, wanting things to be a certain way and feeling like your well-being or sense of being okay depends on things being that way?

_____

_____

_____

_____

The second truth is an invitation to let go of contingency—to accept things as they are in the moment and to not define yourself by the things that you do or do not have (this includes material things and experiences). This notion of self-agency was a radical one twenty-five hundred years ago. While it is generally accepted today, this message of personal responsibility is still a radical one. We fabricate our experience out of stories and desires. If we can revise the stories, our desires can change. This gives us a clue about the third noble truth—how to bring all this self-induced trouble to an end.

Third Noble Truth: The Truth of the End of Dukkha

The Buddha's teaching was very optimistic. We can make a difference in what we experience. We can train our minds through wisdom, ethics, and meditation so that we don't perpetuate suffering. When the internal mind chatter stops, when the grasping after things ends, and when we no longer strain to push things away, our minds will be at peace. Desire, aversion, and confusion (about the nature of self and reality) stop. These forces of desire and confusion obscure us from our natural experience that is one of deep, abiding peace, tranquillity, serenity, bliss, and contentment—similar to an introverted perspective on happiness. Equanimity, love, compassion, and joy are also present. The Buddha didn't jump up and down for joy, he didn't shout how happy he was—he just embodied that presence. This is the truth of nirvana. Like dukkha, nirvana is a metaphor. *Nirvana* means cessation. It is like a fire going out because there is no more fuel to burn. It is not some destination or attainment. Nirvana is present all the time, but we can't experience it until we cease from our identifying with thoughts, clinging to possessions, and pursuing other things we feel we must have or control.

There is an end to introvert-related anguish when you can self-empower through insights, self-care, and setting limits on extrovert demands. When you can embrace the teachings of the Buddha and set limits on your own expectations and the expectations of the extroverts around you, you put yourself in a better position to live more freely and fully. The introvert's version of nirvana is a comfort within your own skin. It is a feeling of spaciousness that you can bring into any situation. You are present to whatever arises and you don't feel burdened by the situation. You feel at home.

Can you remember a moment when you didn't want things to be other than they were? How did you feel? This may have been a taste of nirvana.

_____

_____

_____

_____

_____

Fourth Noble Truth: The Path to the Cessation of Dukkha

The fourth noble truth outlines a comprehensive path for awakening known as the "eightfold path." It is comprised of three themes: wisdom, ethics, and meditation. The path is often compared to a wheel, with each facet of the path—right view, right resolve, right speech, right action, right livelihood, right effort, right mindfulness, right concentration—comprising a spoke of that wheel. No one facet is superior to the others, and all are needed for the wheel to work. Note that these *rights* are not moral injunctions but rather practical ones. If you engage in harmful activities, this creates disruptive patterns of thoughts and emotions, and leads to further harmful actions. It's hard, if not impossible, to maintain the focus required for meditation if these kinds of disruptions are happening. When you understand what is at stake through right view, you'll also be disinclined to generate such harmful intentions and actions. This is a very different approach to morality than the more familiar "thou shalts" and "thou shalt nots." Ethics is a self-empowering practice guided by wisdom, concern for others, and skillful honing of attention.

The activities of the eightfold path are done within a context of understanding that you are different from the extroverts around you and are not deficient in comparison to them. Along with this comprehension is a resolve to change things: to be an empowered and awakened introvert. Mindfulness is at the heart of this transformation process.

Now that an introvert revolution is taking place, as evidenced by the explosion of writing, interest, and advocacy for introversion, you can awaken to your preferred style without apology. You can embrace your introversion without conforming. There are two levels to consider: the relative world of self and narrative and the transcendent world of deep awakening. The self-affirmations of the introvert revolution can help you to be more comfortable at the level of self and narrative. Of course, you may wish to transcend this narrative sense of self through a serious meditation practice. Being comfortable with your introversion will be a stronger launching point for the deeper spirituality.

Right View

The path has to start with some understanding. Like Siddhartha, you have to know you are in trouble before you can start to seek a solution. You have to know that something is off—that life is suffused with dukkha—and that you have something to do with this. This is *right view.* By "right," the Buddha did not mean right or wrong in the moralistic sense. He meant right as in *correct* or *true*, like a wheel that rolls true. (Remember the metaphor for dukkha was a broken wheel—in other words, a wheel that is not *true*.)

An introvert-specific version of right view seeks to understand the relationship between personality, what is self, and what is not self. It appreciates how introverts live in the world differently in terms of how they handle attention, energy, and stimulation. Right view combines knowledge with acceptance. There is an acceptance of your introversion that can become a celebration of your unique gifts. Right view is up to speed on how your brain is already stimulated and therefore needs less stimulation. It knows that you love people and feel connected with people *and* that you want to be alone sometimes, maybe even often.

Sit with this definition of right view for a few moments and reflect on how this fits for you. What does it mean to you to be an introvert? How do you see yourself moving forward with this understanding? What can you add?

Right Resolve

Once right view is established, you need to make a decision. It is possible to know something is wrong but not be ready to act on that knowledge. There must be a resolution to act, and this brings you to the second spoke on this true wheel: *right resolve*. Right resolve is a commitment to living skillfully—that is, with intelligence and a commitment to do what is beneficial. Skillful introversion is unapologetic and mindful of the values and pitfalls of being introverted. The resolute introvert is committed to self-care by nurturing energy, exploring the interior with discernment, and providing ample opportunities for solitude.

Sit with this definition of right resolve for a few moments and reflect on how this fits for you. How do you see yourself moving forward with this resolve? What are you committed to in honor of yourself as an introvert?

Right Speech

With right view and resolve in place, you are ready to act in the world. These actions can either help or hinder your progress on the path. What you say, how you treat others, and what you do in the world comprise the scope of ethical activities. *Right speech* counsels that what comes out of your mouth should be truthful and also beneficial. The Buddha also advised against idle chatter and gossip, because they divert attention away from what is important and, in the case of gossip, can lead to harm.

Right speech is speech that does not harm. Say what is true and beneficial. Aim to be intentional with your words. Since uttering such words takes energy, and is not done just for the sake of making small talk, seek to make your words count. Listen first, speak second. Think before you speak. This should come naturally to you. Be patient when you are interrupted. Breathe and wait for your chance, even if that chance is silence.

Sit with this definition of right speech for a few moments and reflect on how this fits for you. What changes would you like to make to your speech patterns?

_____

_____

_____

_____

Right Action

You must also be mindful of the impact of your actions, aiming to minimize the harm that you do to others, the world, and yourself. This is *right action*. As an introvert, you are conscientious about your impact on others, as reflected in your speech tendencies (for example, listening more than talking). You don't like to call attention to yourself, and you are prone to think through the implications of your words, decisions, and actions.

Because of your tendency to become overstimulated, you need to avoid the opposite tendency: stagnation. Right action for the introvert also keeps your body in motion through a balance of contemplation and movement. There are many ways to move with mindfulness (any movement can be mindful when you bring attention to it). Many contemplative practices fuse movement and mindfulness, such as walking meditation (see chapter 7), yoga, qigong, and tai chi.

Sit with this definition of right action for a few moments and reflect on how this fits for you. What actions are you happy with? What needs improvement? Are you moving enough? If not, how can you incorporate more movement into your life?

_____

_____

_____

_____

Right Livelihood

Right livelihood focuses on what you do for work. Here again, harm should not be caused and the work you do should benefit others. If you make weapons of mass destruction, you are not practicing right livelihood.

Right livelihood has integrity, honesty, and beneficence and, for introverts, also self-care. If you have sought work that abides with your nature, such as work that involves solitude and meaningful contact with people, you are bound to be happier. If you have sought work that helps people even as it puts you in extroverted roles, such as health care professional, educator, or actor, you have a greater challenge. If you work in a role that is unrelentingly extroverted with no time for recovery, you will be at a great disadvantage. If you work in a space without privacy, quiet, or time for introspection, then you will have to deliberately counteract the adverse effects of this environment. For many introverts, their livelihood comes with a high price tag. If you are one of these, you will have to embrace the exercises throughout this book to help keep you on track. It may also be worth considering whether this taxing work accords with your deepest values. If it doesn't, then consider other options for contributing to the world. Can you give yourself permission to give to the world without sacrificing your own well-being?

Sit with this definition of right livelihood for a few moments and reflect on how this fits for you. Do you need to make any changes in the way you work? Can you give yourself permission to do so?

_____

_____

_____

_____

Right Effort

The Buddha valued meditation, and the final three components of the path—right effort, right mindfulness, and right concentration—guide the process of going within. It is hard work to change the mental habits of a lifetime, and if this effort is not done with wisdom, it can further bad habits. If you strive too hard to be mindful—for instance, if your meditation is done compulsively with ample doses of self-criticism for any missed sessions or for any meditations that fall short of some preconceived notion of what the meditation should feel like—you miss the point. You meditate a lot, but you do so with a joyless tightness. That would not be right effort. *Right effort* brings commitment to the process without attachment to the results. You need to strike a balance between making the effort to practice without becoming identified with those efforts. It's easy to become a "meditator," but this is not really the point. The goal is to use meditation as a tool for awakening. You also have to apply effort to managing your energy (see chapter 6). Effort aims to move energy in the "right" direction, by being true to your aspirations to be more mindful, effective, and awake.

Sit with this definition of right effort for a few moments and reflect on how this fits for you. How do you see yourself making efforts in the short and long term?

_____

_____

_____

_____

Right Mindfulness

Right mindfulness seeks to orient attention to the present moment. Mindfulness requires letting go of the stories of "I, me, and mine." Mindfulness turns to the body as a refuge. Mindfulness is the skill of staying connected to experience and recovering from getting lost in stories, strong emotions, and interpersonal dramas. Mindfulness is the glue that holds all the other noble truths together. Right mindfulness is attention to the present moment without attachment or aversion. Mindfulness brings along with it many other mental factors, such as a wish to not harm yourself or others. Mindfulness is tranquil, malleable, and wieldy. Right mindfulness is letting go into this moment without agenda, self-reference, or fear.

Sit with this definition of right mindfulness for a few moments and reflect on how this fits for you. What gets in the way of you being mindful? When you are mindful, how do you feel? Have you felt tranquillity and other factors such as the desire to not harm?

_____

_____

_____

_____

Right Concentration

Right mindfulness gives rise to *right concentration*, which brings peace, clarity, and insight. True concentration is more than being focused. It is the ability to access profound states of consciousness. As an introvert, you have a predilection toward concentration, preferring to do one thing at a time without interruption. You can harness this capacity to practice meditation on a daily basis and on extended silent retreats.

Sit with this definition of right concentration for a few moments and reflect on how this fits for you. Can you recall a recent time when you were able to engage deep concentration? What did you notice? How can you leverage your concentration toward self-knowledge?

_____

_____

_____

_____

Rolling the Wheel

Each of these "rights" or "trues" comprises a spoke on the wheel of life. Each spoke is required to make the wheel roll true. Each is essential and indispensable and interacts with one another (see figure).

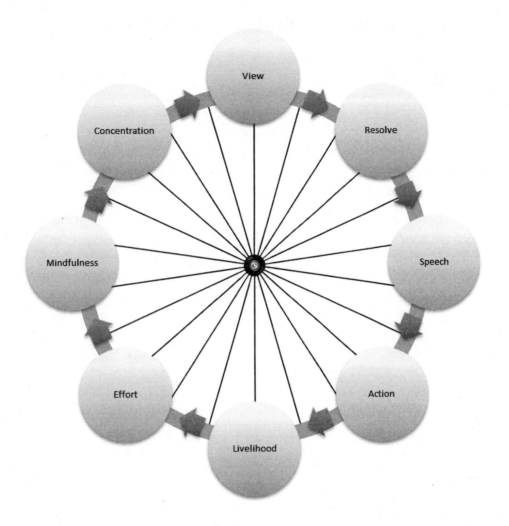

First, there is view. Nothing can happen without this intellectual grounding. Next, you must have a resolve to act, a resolve to change your state and then make the effort to bring it about. Then you must monitor your progress through the wheel's various spokes with mindful, conscious attention. When you move off course, you can simply (and without acrimony) come back and try again. The following form can help you organize your efforts on this path. From your reflections in the preceding sections, fill in the form. What are your commitments to each of the features of the path? How will you know when you are successful?

Eightfold Path Commitments

Feature	Commitments	Success
Right View		
Right Resolve		
Right Speech		
Right Action		
Right Livelihood		
Right Effort		
Right Mindfulness		
Right Concentration		

Formal Meditation: *The Buddha Was an Introvert*

This guided visualization will help you to embrace your introverted Buddha-nature. The image of the Buddha sitting serenely, unperturbed by the rising and falling of thoughts, emotions, and events, can help guide you to your own vision of how you'd like your life to be. The Buddha does not apologize for his appetite for quiet, solitude, and peace. He knows that it is essential to embrace these strategies. Like the Buddha, you can carry solitude with you and access it whenever you drop into the sensations of your body. Like the Buddha, you carry quiet with you whenever you can disengage the mind from inner commentary and be in the moment as it is without adding anything. Like the Buddha, you have reserves of energy that are nurtured by meditation practice and the wisdom of seeing things clearly and not resisting reality. Acceptance is the doorway to this moment. Walk through it often.

The Buddha knew that quiet, solitude, and energy are qualities that are nurtured by an intelligent approach to life. He knew that mindfulness is a beautiful mental factor, embodying tranquillity and a lack of grasping desire or aversion. At the same time, mindfulness fosters a profound affection for self and others, a wish not to harm. The Buddha arranged his life to prioritize meditation and time for rest and recovery. The Buddha spoke from compassion for others and retired to recharge, motivated by self-compassion. The Buddha knew himself and endeavored to keep exploring. He was always smiling a half smile, and he knew that happiness arose from within and not from external conditions. You are the Buddha, too, and each cycle of the breath that you take with awareness moves you a little closer to embracing this Buddha-nature.

Get into a comfortable posture and set your intention to practice. Shift your attention from the internal workings of the mind to your body. Feel your breath moving in the body and rest your attention there. As you breathe, you anchor yourself in the present moment. Spend a few minutes here, connecting to your breathing body. As you do this, notice how everything is changing in every moment. No two breaths are identical; no two sensations arise in precisely the same way. Notice how your mind's excursions into commentary on the future, past, or present give rise to some emotion, often a negative one. If you examine these feelings, you'll notice that they are an almost constant presence in the background of awareness. This background "radiation" is the activity of dukkha—the pervasive sense of suffering, dissatisfaction, and anguish that besets the mind. Something feels off and the mind wants to "fix" it. When you return attention to the breath in the moment, the conditions that give rise to that offness cease for an instant and you arrive in the present moment. If you keep looking, you will notice that your sense of "me" is just like your emotions; it is prompted by the activity of the mind. Your sense of identity gets solidified and maintained by memories and by projecting into the future. Self is confirmed by every opinion that the mind holds.

Picture yourself sitting in meditation like the Buddha. Embrace his peace, serenity, and wisdom. Remind yourself that you, too, have the capacity to awaken, and therefore, you are a Buddha, too. Whether you are sitting alone or with a group, you are connected to people all over the world who are also exploring their inner landscapes. You are practicing being alone together with others, both close and remote.

Meditation Reflection

Take a few moments to contemplate this practice. Were you able to get relief from the tendency to "fix" things, even if only for a moment? Were you able to notice the difference between generating more of this background radiation and resting peacefully in the present moment?

_____

_____

_____

_____

Concluding Thoughts: The Buddha's Introvert Legacy

We don't know for sure whether the Buddha was an introvert or an extrovert. If he was an introvert, he may have had to act like an extrovert as many introverts do, especially during the first three decades of his life. Whether or not he would have scored as an introvert on today's personality measurements, he advocated an introverted path toward the pinnacle of self-expression: awakening. He brought thousands of people together to sit in communal silence—alone and with others. He advocated a method for introspection that simultaneously reveals reality as it is and protects the meditator from getting caught up in painful internal stories. Mindfulness was key to his method. His legacy can be seen around the world through the Buddhist religions and, in the West, in secular forms such as mindfulness-based stress reduction, which has permeated health care, the armed forces, corporations, and education. Research is beginning to confirm many of the Buddha's observations and the value of mindfulness-based approaches.

Everyone has an introvert aspect that can move toward awakening, and it is not only introverts who show up to do Buddhist-style meditation. The hectic pace of modern life and the constant noise from digital technology create stress for everyone, introverts and extroverts alike. We are all best served when we can value and access our introvert qualities while also being able to behave like an extrovert in selected situations.

The Buddha embodied the extroverted teacher, giving thousands of lectures during his long teaching career of forty-five years. He balanced these extroverted forays in teaching with dedicated time in silent meditation that served his introvert needs. This formula can work well for introverts today just as it did twenty-five centuries ago. Each time you practice mindfulness, you are touching your inner Buddha, your Buddha-nature, and moving just a little bit closer to awakening. Be like the Buddha and sit alone with others. Nurture the interior connection—this is the introvert way. Be the guardian of your own solitude by committing to daily mindfulness practice to thrive in your life.

Afterword

Congratulations! You have reached the end of this workbook and have made steps toward becoming an awakened introvert. Your increased self-knowledge, self-empowerment, and mindfulness skills can change the way that you live in the world. Instead of being at the mercy of extrovert demands, you can navigate the landscapes of relationships and work by setting limits where needed, expanding your boundaries where judicious, and engaging in restorative self-care every day.

You have awakened to your introvert potential and you have been introduced to the path to wider awakening that has mindfulness at its heart. To awaken is to come out of self-imposed limitations. To awaken is also to transcend some biological programming. You don't have to be a slave to every impulse that arises. These impulses served human ancestors eons ago, but you can make different choices today. While you *can* think all the time, you can also choose not to.

The exercises in this workbook have been designed to introduce, illustrate, and inspire new habits for you. You, no doubt, have some favorites and I encourage you to stick with them, especially the mindfulness meditation practices. Your awakening process will continue to unfold the more you practice and the more you embrace the principles of introvert self-care you have learned so far. Quiet, solitude, and energy-restoring rest can now be a nurtured part of your life. Armed with a better understanding of your unique needs and strengths, as well as more skills for leveraging mindfulness for your awakening, you can flourish in your life like never before. You now have a set of tools you can take with you for a lifetime. Use them often and enjoy happiness, well-being, and peace.

Resources

Recordings and Books by Arnie Kozak, PhD

Mindfulness Meditation Recordings

The Exquisite Mind website has ten hours of guided meditation recordings that you can listen to and download for free (http://www.exquisitemind.com). You can also visit this website for information on upcoming workshops that Arnie Kozak teaches at the Kripalu Center for Yoga and Health, the Barre Center for Buddhist Studies, and the Copper Beech Institute.

Arnie also writes two blogs: *Mindfulness Matters* (http://www.beliefnet.com/columnists/mindfulnessmatters/) and *The Awakened Introvert* on Quiet Revolution (http://www.quietrev.com).

Books

The Everything Buddhism Book. 2nd edition. Avon, MA: Adams Media Corporation, 2011.

The Everything Essential Buddhism Book. Avon, MA: Adams Media Corporation, 2015.

The Everything Guide to the Introvert Edge. Avon, MA: Adams Media Corporation, 2013.

Meditation Made Simple: Seven Considerations to Get You Started. Burlington, VT: Exquisite Mind Press, 2014. (Available as an e-book.)

Mindfulness A–Z: 108 Insights for Awakening Now. Boston: Wisdom Publications, 2015.

Overcoming Obstacles to Practice. Burlington, VT: Exquisite Mind Press, 2014. (Available as an e-book.)

Swing Like You Don't Care: Mindfulness for Golf and Golf as a Spiritual Path. Burlington, VT: Exquisite Mind Press, 2014. (Available as an e-book.)

Wild Chickens and Petty Tyrants: 108 Metaphors for Mindfulness. Boston: Wisdom Publications, 2009.

Additional Reading

Introvert Books

Ancowitz, Nancy. *Self-Promotion for Introverts: The Quiet Guide to Getting Ahead.* New York: McGraw Hill, 2009.

Aron, Elaine. *The Highly Sensitive Person: How to Survive When the World Overwhelms You.* New York: Broadway Books, 1997.

Cain, Susan. *Quiet: The Power of Introverts in a World That Can't Stop Talking.* New York: Broadway Books, 2013.

Chung, Michaela. *Introvert Revolution: A Quiet Path to Reclaiming Our Power.* Amazon Digital Services, 2013.

Dembling, Sophia. *The Introvert's Way: Living a Quiet Life in a Noisy World.* New York: Perigee, 2012.

Helgoe, Laurie. *Introvert Power: Why Your Inner Life Is Your Hidden Strength.* New York: Source-books, 2013.

Kahnweiler, Jennifer. *The Introverted Leader: Building on Your Quiet Strength.* San Francisco: Berrett-Koehler Publishers, 2009.

———. *Quiet Influence: The Introvert's Guide to Making a Difference.* San Francisco: Berrett-Koehler Publishers, 2013.

Laney, Marti Olsen. *The Hidden Gifts of the Introverted Child*. New York: Workman, 2005.

———. *The Introvert Advantage: How to Thrive in an Extrovert World*. New York: Workman, 2002.

———. *The Introvert and Extrovert in Love: Making It Work When Opposites Attract*. Oakland, CA: New Harbinger Publications, 2007.

McHugh, Adam. *Introverts in the Church: Finding Our Place in an Extroverted Culture*. Downers Grove, IL: IVP Books, 2009.

Okerlund, Nancy. *Introverts at Ease: An Insider's Guide to a Great Life on Your Terms*. North Charleston, SC: CreateSpace, 2011.

Petrilli, Lisa. *The Introvert's Guide to Success in Business and Leadership*. C-Level Strategies, 2011.

Wagele, Elizabeth. *The Happy Introvert: A Wild and Crazy Guide to Celebrating Your True Self*. Berkeley, CA: Ulysses Press, 2006.

Zack, Devora. *Networking for People Who Hate Networking: A Field Guide for Introverts, the Overwhelmed, and the Underconnected*. San Francisco: Berrett-Koehler Publishers, 2010.

Mindfulness, Buddhism, and Related Books

Batchelor, Stephen. *Buddhism Without Beliefs*. New York: Riverhead, 1998.

———. *Confession of a Buddhist Atheist*. New York: Spiegel and Grau, 2011.

Bernhard, Toni. *How to Wake Up: A Buddhist-Inspired Guide to Navigating Joy and Sorrow*. Boston: Wisdom Publications, 2013.

———. *How to Be Sick: A Buddhist-Inspired Guide for the Chronically Ill and Their Caregivers*. Boston: Wisdom Publications, 2010.

Boccio, Frank Jude. *Mindfulness Yoga*. Boston: Wisdom Publications, 2004.

Bodhi, Bikkhu. *The Noble Eightfold Path: The Way to the End of Suffering*. Kandy, Sri Lanka: Buddhist Publication Society, 1994.

Boorstein, Sylvia. *It's Easier than You Think: The Buddhist Way to Happiness*. San Francisco: HarperOne, 1997.

Brach, Tara. *Radical Acceptance: Embracing Your Life with the Heart of a Buddha*. New York: Bantam, 2003.

———. *True Refuge: Finding Peace and Freedom in Your Own Awakened Heart*. New York: Bantam, 2012.

Brantley, Jeffrey. *Calming Your Anxious Mind: How Mindfulness and Compassion Can Free You from Anxiety, Fear, and Panic*. Oakland, CA: New Harbinger Publications, 2007.

Cameron, Julia. *The Artist's Way*. New York: Tarcher, 2002.

Chödrön, Pema. *The Places That Scare You*. Boston: Shambhala, 2007.

———. *When Things Fall Apart*. Boston: Shambhala, 2000.

Chozen-Bays, Jan. *How to Train a Wild Elephant and Other Adventures in Mindfulness*. Boston. Shambhala, 2011.

———. *Mindful Eating: A Guide to Rediscovering a Healthy and Joyful Relationship with Food*. Boston: Shambhala, 2009.

Epstein, Mark. *Going on Being: Life at the Crossroads of Buddhism and Psychotherapy*. New York: Broadway Books, 2001.

———. *Thoughts Without a Thinker*. New York: Basic Books, 1995.

———. *The Trauma of Everyday Life*. New York: Penguin, 2013.

Flowers, Stephen. *The Mindful Path Through Shyness*. Oakland, CA: New Harbinger Publications, 2009.

Goldberg, Natalie. *Writing Down the Bones*. Boston: Shambhala, 1986.

Goldstein, Elisha. *Mindfulness Meditations for the Anxious Traveler: Quick Exercises to Calm Your Mind*. New York: Atria, 2012.

———. *The Now Effect*. New York: Atria, 2012.

———. *Uncovering Happiness: Overcoming Depression with Mindfulness and Self-Compassion*. New York: Atria, 2015.

Goldstein, Joseph. *The Experience of Insight*. Boston: Shambhala, 1983.

———. *Insight Meditation: The Practice of Freedom*. Boston: Shambhala, 2003.

———. *Mindfulness: A Practical Guide to Awakening*. Boulder: Sounds True, 2013.

———. *One Dharma: The Emerging Western Buddhism*. San Francisco: HarperCollins, 2011.

Goldstein, Joseph, and Jack Kornfield. *Seeking the Heart of Wisdom*. Boston: Shambhala, 2001.

Gombrich, Richard. *What the Buddha Thought*. London, England: Equinox, 2009.

Gunaratana, Bhante. *Beyond Mindfulness in Plain English: An Introductory Guide to Deeper States of Meditation*. Boston: Wisdom Publications, 2009.

———. *Mindfulness in Plain English*. Boston: Wisdom Publications, 2002.

Harris, Dan. *10% Happier: How I Tamed the Voice in My Head, Reduced Stress Without Losing My Edge, and Found Self-Help That Actually Works—A True Story*. New York: It Books, 2014.

Kabat-Zinn, Jon. *Arriving at Your Own Door: 108 Lessons in Mindfulness*. New York: Hyperion, 2007.

———. *Coming to Our Senses*. New York: Hyperion, 2005.

———. *Full Catastrophe Living*. New York: Delta, 1990.

———. *Wherever You Go, There You Are*. New York: Hyperion, 1994.

Kaza, Stephanie. *Hooked!: Buddhist Writings on Greed, Desire, and the Urge to Consume*. Boston: Shambhala, 2005.

———. *Mindfully Green: A Personal and Spiritual Guide to Whole Earth Thinking*. Boston: Shambhala, 2011.

Kornfield, Jack. *After the Ecstasy, the Laundry*. New York: Bantam, 2000.

———. *A Path with Heart*. New York: Bantam, 1993.

———. *The Wise Heart*. New York: Bantam, 2008.

Kramer, Gregory. *Insight Dialogue: The Interpersonal Path to Freedom*. Boston: Shambhala, 2007.

Levine, Noah. *Against the Stream*. San Francisco: HarperCollins, 2007.

———. *Dharma Punx*. San Francisco: HarperCollins, 2003.

Nhat Hanh, Thich. *Being Peace*. Berkeley, CA: Parallax Press, 2005.

———. *The Miracle of Mindfulness*. Boston: Beacon, 1996.

Olendzki, Andrew. *Unlimiting Mind: The Radically Experiential Psychology of Buddhism*. Boston: Wisdom Publications, 2010.

Rahula, Wahula. *What the Buddha Taught*. New York: Grove Press, 1974.

Rinzler, Lodro. *The Buddha Walks Into a Bar… A Guide to Life for a New Generation*. Boston: Shambhala, 2012.

Rosenberg, Larry. *Breath by Breath: The Liberating Practice of Insight Meditation*. Boston: Shambhala, 1998.

———. *Living in the Light of Death*. Boston: Shambhala, 2000.

Rosenberg, Larry, and Laura Zimmerman. *Three Steps to Awakening: A Practice for Bringing Mindfulness to Life*. Boston: Shambhala, 2013.

Salzberg, Sharon. *A Heart as Wide as the World*. Boston: Shambhala, 1997.

———. *Lovingkindness*. Boston: Shambhala, 2002.

———. *Real Happiness: The Power of Meditation*. New York: Workman, 2010.

Segal, Zindel V., J. Mark Williams, and John D. Teasdale. *Mindfulness-Based Cognitive Therapy for Depression: A New Approach to Preventing Relapse*. New York: Guilford Press, 2002.

Siegel, Daniel J. *The Mindful Brain*. New York: W. W. Norton, 2007.

———. *Mindful Therapist: A Clinician's Guide to Mindsight and Neural Integration*. New York: W. W. Norton, 2010.

———. *Mindsight: The New Science of Personal Transformation*. New York: Bantam, 2010.

Smith, Rodney. *Awakening: A Paradigm Shift for the Heart*. Boston: Shambhala, 2014.

———. *Stepping Out of Self-Deception: The Buddha's Liberating Teaching of No-Self.* Boston: Shambhala, 2011.

Soeng, Mu. *The Heart of the Universe: Exploring the Heart Sutra.* Boston: Wisdom Publications, 2010.

Stahl, Bob, and Elisha Goldstein. *The Mindfulness-Based Stress Reduction Workbook.* Oakland, CA: New Harbinger Publications, 2010.

Trungpa, Chogyam. *Cutting Through Spiritual Materialism.* Boston: Shambhala, 2002.

———. *The Myth of Freedom.* Boston: Shambhala, 2002.

Whyte, David. *Crossing the Unknown Sea: Work as a Pilgrimage of Identity.* New York: Riverhead, 2002.

———. *The Heart Aroused: Poetry and Preservation of the Soul in Corporate America.* New York: Crown Business, 2002.

———. *The Three Marriages: Reimagining Work, Self, and Relationship.* New York: Riverhead, 2010.

Williams, Mark, John Teasdale, Zindel Segal, and Jon Kabat-Zinn. *The Mindful Way Through Depression.* New York: Guilford Press, 2007.

Yogis, Jaimal. *The Fear Project: What Our Most Primal Emotion Taught Me About Survival, Success, Surfing...and Love.* New York: Rodale, 2013.

———. *Saltwater Buddha: A Surfer's Quest to Find Zen on the Sea.* Boston: Wisdom Publications, 2009.

Young-Eisendrath, Polly. *The Present Heart: A Memoir of Love, Loss, and Discovery.* New York: Rodale, 2014.

———. *The Self-Esteem Trap: Raising Confident Kids in an Age of Self-Importance.* New York: Little Brown, 2009.

Poetry

Barrows, Anita. *Rilke's Book of Hours: Love Poems to God.* New York: Riverhead, 2005.

Berry, Wendell. *The Selected Poems of Wendell Berry.* Berkeley, CA: Counterpoint, 1999.

Eliot, T. S. *Collected Poems.* Orlando, FL: Harcourt Brace, 1963.

———. *Four Quartets.* New York: Harvest, 1971.

Emerson, Ralph Waldo. *Collected Poems and Translations*. New York: Penguin, 1994.

Hafiz. *The Gift*. Translated by D. Ladinski. New York: Penguin, 1999.

Kabir. *Ecstatic Poems*. Translated by R. Bly. Boston: Beacon, 2004.

Kinnell, Galway. *A New Selected Poems*. New York: Houghton Mifflin, 2000.

Lao-tzu. *The Way of Life*. Translated by W. Bynner. New York: Penguin, 1944.

Merwin, W. S. *Migration: New and Selected Poems*. Port Townsend, WA: Copper Canyon Press, 2007.

————. *The Shadow of Sirius*. Port Townsend, WA: Copper Canyon Press, 2009.

Mitchell, Stephen. *The Selected Poetry of Rainer Maria Rilke*. New York: Vintage, 1989.

Mood, John J. L. *Rilke on Love and Other Difficulties*. New York: W. W. Norton, 1994.

Nelson, Portia. *There's a Hole in My Sidewalk: The Romance of Self-Discovery*. Hillsboro, OR: Beyond Words, 1993.

Oliver, Mary. *New and Selected Poems*. Boston: Beacon Books, 1992.

Rilke, Rainer Maria. *Letters to a Young Poet*. Translated by J. Burnham. Novato, CA: New World Library, 2000.

Rumi. *The Soul of Rumi*. Translated by C. Barks. San Francisco: HarperCollins, 2001.

Szymborska, Wiclava. *View with a Grain of Sand*. New York: Harcourt Brace, 1995.

Walcott, D. *Collected Poems*. New York: Farrar, Straus and Giroux,1987.

Whyte, David. *Everything Is Waiting for You*. Langley, WA: Many Rivers Press, 2003.

————. *The Fire in the Earth*. Langley, WA: Many Rivers Press, 1992.

————. *The House of Belonging*. Langley, WA: Many Rivers Press, 1997.

————. *Pilgrim*. Langley, WA: Many Rivers Press, 2012.

———. *River Flow*. Langley, WA: Many Rivers Press, 2012.

———. *Songs for Coming Home*. Langley, WA: Many Rivers Press, 1989.

———. *Where Many Rivers Meet*. Langley, WA: Many Rivers Press, 1990.

Major Retreat Centers

East Coast: Insight Meditation Society, http://www.dharma.org

West Coast: Spirit Rock, http://www.spiritrock.org

Mindfulness Resources

Barre Center for Buddhist Studies, http://www.bcbsdharma.org

Cambridge Insight Meditation Center, http://www.cimc.info/index.html

Center for Mindfulness in Medicine, Health Care, and Society, http://www.umassmed.edu/cfm

Elisha Goldstein, http://elishagoldstein.com

eMindful, http://emindful.com

Mindful Awareness Research Center (MARC), http://marc.ucla.edu

Mindsight Institute, http://www.mindsightinstitute.com

Shinzen Young, http://www.shinzen.org

Tara Brach, http://www.tarabrach.com

Tricycle magazine, http://www.tricycle.org
    The magazine hosts an online community. With a membership, you can access articles, online retreats, and film.

UCLA Mind and Life Institute, http://www.mindandlife.org

References

Abram, Jan. 2007. *The Language of Winnicott: A Dictionary of Winnicott's Use of Words*. London: Karnac.

Aron, Elaine. 1997. *The Highly Sensitive Person: How to Survive When the World Overwhelms You*. New York: Broadway Books.

Barrows, Anita. 2005. *Rilke's Book of Hours: Love Poems to God*. New York: Riverhead.

Ben-Shahar, Tal. 2007. *Happier: Learn the Secrets to Joy and Daily Fulfillment*. New York: McGraw-Hill.

Bhikku, Thanissaro. 1996. *The Wings to Awakening*. Barre, MA: Dhamma Dana Publications.

Blumenthal, Terry D. 2001. "Extraversion, Attention, and Startle Reactivity." *Personality and Individual Differences* 30: 495–503.

Brahm, Ajahn. 2014. *Don't Worry, Be Grumpy: Inspiring Stories for Making the Most of Each Moment*. Boston: Wisdom Publications.

Brewer, Judson. 2011. "Meditation Experience Is Associated with Differences in Default Mode Network Activity and Connectivity." *PNAS* 108: 20254–59.

Brown, Brené. 2010. *The Gifts of Imperfection*. Center City, MN: Hazelden.

Cain, Susan. 2012. *Quiet: The Power of Introverts in a World That Can't Stop Talking*. New York: Crown.

Chung, Michaela. 2013. *Introvert Revolution: A Quiet Path for Reclaiming Our Power*.

Dembling, Sophia. 2012. *The Introvert's Way: Living a Quiet Life in a Noisy World*. New York: Perigee.

de Mello, Anthony. 2010. *Seek God Everywhere: Reflections on the Spiritual Exercises of St. Ignatius*. New York: Image/Doubleday.

Dietrich, Maria, and Katherine V. Abbot. 2012. "Vocal Function in Introverts and Extraverts During a Psychological Stress Reactivity Protocol." *Journal of Speech, Language, and Hearing Research* 55: 973–87.

Eliot, T. S. 1968. *Four Quartets*. New York: Mariner.

Emerson, Ralph Waldo. 1993. *Self-Reliance and Other Essays*. New York: Dover.

Epstein, Mark. 2013. *The Trauma of Everyday Life*. New York: Penguin.

Evans, Richard I. 1964. *Conversations with Carl Jung and Reactions from Ernest Jones*. Princeton, NJ: D. Van Norstrand.

Fleeson, William, and Patrick Gallagher. 2009. "The Implications of Big Five Standing for the Distribution of Trait Manifestation in Behavior: Fifteen Experience-Sampling Studies and a Meta-Analysis." *Journal of Personality and Social Psychology* 97: 1097–1114.

Forsman, Lea J., Orjan de Manzano, Anke Karabanov, Guy Madison, and Fredrik Ullen. 2012. "Differences in Regional Brain Volume Related to the Extraversion-Introversion Dimension—A Voxel-Based Morphometric Study." *Neuroscience Research* 72: 59–67.

Furnham, Adrian, Joanna Moutafi, and John Crump. 2003. "The Relationship Between the Revised NEO Personality Inventory and the Myers-Briggs Type Indicator." *Social Behavior and Personality* 31: 577–84.

Gibran, Kahlil. 1969. *The Prophet*. New York: Knopf.

Goldberg, Natalie. 1986. *Writing Down the Bones*. Boston: Shambhala.

Goleman, Daniel. 2013. *Focus: The Hidden Driver of Excellence*. New York: Harper.

Gombrich, Richard. 2009. *What the Buddha Thought*. London: Equinox.

Gosling, Samuel D., Peter J. Rentfrow, and William B. Swann Jr. 2003. "A Very Brief Measure of the Big-Five Personality Domains." *Journal of Research in Personality* 37: 504–28.

Hartley, Jenny, ed. 2012. *The Selected Letters of Charles Dickens*. Oxford, England: Oxford University Press.

Helgoe, Laurie. 2013. *Introvert Power: Why Your Inner Life is Your Hidden Strength*. Naperville, IL: Sourcebooks.

Hills, Peter, and Michael Argyle. 2001. "Happiness, Introversion-Extraversion and Happy Introverts." *Personality and Individual Differences* 30: 595–608.

Johnson, Debra, John Weibe, and Sherri Gold. 1999. "Cerebral Blood Flow and Personality: A Positron Emission Tomography Study. *American Journal of Psychiatry* 156: 252–57.

Kabat-Zinn, Jon. 1990. *Full Catastrophe Living: Using the Wisdom of Your Body and Mind to Face Stress, Pain, and Illness*. New York: Delta.

Kim, Jungsoo, and Richard de Dear. 2013. "Workspace Satisfaction: The Privacy-Communication Trade-Off in Open-Plan Offices." *Journal of Environmental Psychology* 36: 18–26.

Lamott. Anne. 2013. *Stitches: A Handbook on Meaning, Hope, and Repair*. New York: Riverhead.

Laney, Marti Olsen. 2002. *The Introvert Advantage: How to Thrive in an Extrovert World*. New York: Workman.

———. 2007. *The Introvert and Extrovert in Love*. Oakland, CA: New Harbinger Publications.

Lucas, Richard E., and Frank Fujita. 2000. "Factors Influencing the Relation Between Extraversion and Pleasant Affect." *Journal of Personality and Social Psychology* 79: 1039–56.

Mazzucchelli, Trevor G., Robert T. Kane, and Clare S. Rees. 2010. "Behavioral Activation Interventions for Well-Being: A Meta-Analysis." *Journal of Positive Psychology* 5: 105–21.

McGregor, Ian, Dan P. McAdams, Brian R. Little. 2006. "Personal Projects, Life Stories, and Happiness: On Being True to Traits." *Journal of Research in Personality* 40: 551–72.

Nielson, Jared A., Brandon A. Zielinski, Michael A. Ferguson, Janet E. Lainhart, and Jeffrey S. Anderson. 2013. "An Evaluation of the Left-Brain vs. Right-Brain Hypothesis with Resting State Functional Connectivity Magnetic Resonance Imaging." *PLOS One* 8: e71275.

Pascal, Blaise. 1958. *Pascal's Pensées.* New York: Dutton.

Rilke, Rainer Maria. 2006. *Letters on Life: New Prose Translations.* Translated by Ulrich Baer. New York: Modern Library.

Rusting, Cheryl L., and Randy J. Larsen. 1997. "Extraversion, Neuroticism, and Susceptibility to Positive and Negative Affect: A Test of Two Theoretical Models." *Personality and Individual Differences* 22: 607–12.

Salmon, Paul, and Susan Matarese. 2014. "Mindfulness Meditation: Seeking Solitude in Community." In *The Handbook of Solitude: Psychological Perspectives on Social Isolation, Social Withdrawal, and Being Alone,* edited by Robert J. Coplan and Julie C. Bowker, 335–50. New York: Wiley-Blackwell.

Schwartz, Tony. 2013. "Relax! You'll be More Productive." The New York Times. February 9, 2013.

Strack, Fritz, Leonard L. Martin, and Sabine Stepper. 1988. "Inhibiting and Facilitating Conditions of the Human Smile: A Non-Obtrusive Test of the Facial Feedback Hypothesis." *Journal of Personality and Social Psychology* 54: 767–77.

Taylor, Véronique A., Joshua Grant, Véronique Daneault, Geneviève Scavone, Estelle Breton, Sébastien Roffe-Vidal, Jérôme Courtemanche, Anaïs S. Lavarenne, and Mario Beauregard. 2011. "Impact of Mindfulness on the Neural Responses to Emotional Pictures in Experienced and Beginner Meditators." *Neuroimage* 57: 1524–33.

Thoreau, Henry David. 2004. *Walden.* Princeton, NJ: Princeton University Press.

Underhill, Evelyn. 1911. *Mysticism: A Study in the Nature and Development of Man's Spiritual Consciousness.* New York: Dutton.

Xu Shiyong, Peng Danling, Jin Zhen, Liu Hongyang, and Yang Jie. 2005. "Personality and Neurochemicals in the Human Brain: A Preliminary Study Using H MRS." *Chinese Science Bulletin* 50: 2319–22.

Whyte, David. 2009. *The Three Marriages: Reimagining Work, Self, and Relationship.* New York: Riverhead.

Young, Shinzen. 2005. *Break Through Pain: A Step-by-Step Mindfulness Meditation Program for Transforming Chronic and Acute Pain.* Boulder, CO: Sounds True.

Zelenski, John M., Maya S. Santoro, and Deanna C. Whelan. 2012. "Would Introverts Be Better Off if They Acted More Like Extraverts? Exploring Emotional and Cognitive Consequences of Counterdispositional Behavior." *Emotion* 12: 290–303.

Zelenski, John M., Karin Sobocko, and Deanna C. Whelan. 2014. "Introversion, Solitude, and Subjective Well-Being." In *The Handbook of Solitude: Psychological Perspectives on Social Isolation, Social Withdrawal, and Being Alone,* edited by Robert J. Coplan and Julie C. Bowker, 184–202. Boston: Wiley-Blackwell.

Zelenski, John M., Deanna C. Whelan, Logan J. Nealis, Christina M. Besner, Maya S. Santoro, and Jessica E. Wynn. 2013. "Personality and Affective Forecasting: Trait Introverts Underpredict the Hedonic Benefits of Acting Extraverted." *Journal of Personality and Social Psychology* 104: 1092–1108.

Arnie Kozak, PhD, is a psychotherapist, clinical assistant professor in psychiatry at the University of Vermont College of Medicine, and workshop leader at the Barre Center for Buddhist Studies and the Kripalu Center for Yoga and Health. He is author of *Wild Chickens and Petty Tyrants: 108 Metaphors for Mindfulness*, *The Everything Guide to the Introvert Edge*, *The Everything Essential Buddhism Book*, and *Mindfulness A to Z: 108 Insights for Awakening Now*. Arnie is dedicated to translating the Buddha's teachings into readily accessible forms. In the long winters of Northern Vermont when he's not working, he rides the frozen slopes on his snowboard. During the short summers, he golfs. During all seasons, you can find him trail running with his dogs in the foothills of the Green Mountains.

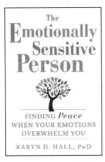
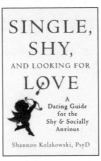

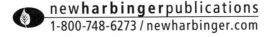

Register your **new harbinger** titles for additional benefits!

When you register your **new harbinger** title—purchased in any format, from any source—you get access to benefits like the following:

- Downloadable accessories like printable worksheets and extra content
- Instructional videos and audio files
- Information about updates, corrections, and new editions

Not every title has accessories, but we're adding new material all the time.

Access free accessories in 3 easy steps:

1. Sign in at NewHarbinger.com (or **register** to create an account).

2. Click on **register a book**. Search for your title and click the **register** button when it appears.

3. Click on the **book cover or title** to go to its details page. Click on **accessories** to view and access files.

That's all there is to it!

If you need help, visit:

NewHarbinger.com/accessories

new harbinger
CELEBRATING
40 YEARS